WHAT GOD HAS JOINED TOGETHER

WHAT GOD HAS JOINED TOGETHER

AN ESSAY ON LOVE

By

GUSTAVE THIBON

LONDON
HOLLIS & CARTER

This translation from the original French, Ce Que Dieu a Uni
(Lardanchet: Paris, 1947), was made by

A. GORDON SMITH

MADE AND PRINTED IN GREAT BRITAIN BY
JARROLD AND SONS LTD., NORWICH, FOR
HOLLIS AND CARTER LTD., 25 ASHLEY PLACE
LONDON, S.W.1

First published 1952

CONTENTS

PART TWO

PREFACE

THE spirit of this book is clearly indicated by its title. There will be found here, with different applications, the same concern for *unity* that inspired my earlier books.

Creation, in its infinite diversity, is a harmonious whole: one in which all the parts are joined and each lives by the rest. From the atom to the angel, from the cohesion of molecules to the communion of saints, nothing exists in isolation or for its own sake alone.

God's act of creation was an act of unifying. The human drama is a drama of separation. Man cuts himself off from God by irreligion; from his brethren by indifference, hatred and war; from his soul by pursuing fugitive and unreal goods. Having separated himself from all else, he reflects his inner discord upon the universe at large; he separates everything about him, lays sacrilegious hands on the humblest traces of divine unity, crumbles up the entrails of matter itself. The atomic bomb is the answer to atomised man.

The metaphysic of separation is the metaphysic of sin. But since man cannot live without the semblance of unity, the various parts of him that sin has disjointed and murdered join up again dead; they are no longer organs of the same body, but grains of sand in the same desert. Separation means confusion,

rupture—and uniformity. There are no more free
and original craftsmen but a "mass" of proletarians;
no more living and responsible leaders but trusts and
departments and totalitarian states; no more lovers
sharing one unique love but standardised beauty
and mechanised sex.

There is only one means of salvation: to return to
unity in diversity. I have tried, in my other books, to
trace the way of such a return in religion and social
relations. I am attempting, here, to review in the
same light the problems of human love.

The four studies that make up the first part of the
book deal with the question in descending degrees of
generality. The first treats of the broad relations
between life and spirit; the second with the connection between sensuous and spiritual love. In the
third I consider marriage, as the total fusion of two
persons and two lives; and in the fourth, the trials
and purifications of love: the ordeals which the love of
man and woman must undergo to gain this indissoluble unity.

The second part is made up of aphorisms: these
gravitate, rather more freely and subjectively, about
the problems already considered.

I have had only one object in publishing these
pages: to help those who are of good will to avoid
putting asunder what God has joined. To this end,
what is most important of all to realise is that no
human fulfilment is possible, even in the purely
temporal order, without seeking its soul and centre
in God.

PART ONE

CHAPTER I

Spirit versus Life

W E will start from facts. Look at humanity, in any age and climate, and you are immediately confronted with conflict. Man might be defined as an animal at war with himself. But what precedes the defining of this human conflict, or any attempt to interpret it, positively or negatively, is the undeniable evidence that it exists.

An animal, like a child, is a simple being. From moment to moment it goes all out for the object that attracts it; each of its acts, one might say, is of a piece. But man is divided; no infallible instinct drives him to his goal; his road is constantly forking, imposing on him the necessity of choice and effort. Combat is at the very heart of his destiny; and every action of his, unlike those of mere cosmic beings, is open to be interpreted as either a victory or a defeat. *Vita hominis militia* . . .

There is a battle taking place every moment of man's life. Where great decisions are involved there is no ignoring that battle; but it is being fought, less conspicuously, in quite trivial circumstances. Teresa of Avila was torn in two between the love of those dearest to her and her love for God; to enter the cloister it cost her the death-throes of her whole nature. Within the soul of the Cid there was war to the death between his passion for duty and the cherished image of Chimène. These were piercing issues, the very thunder of battle! They must not blind us to the minor skirmishes: the battle to shake off sleep in the morning; to resist the April sun, which would have us walk and enjoy it instead of toiling indoors. Tragic conflicts in the grand manner are rare: it is the upshot of these purely trifling combats that gives the soul its definitive form.

But conflict means dualism. The fact of conflict established, it remains to define the opposing forces that confront one another in the human soul. There are plenty of explanations of this human conflict, and each expresses one authentic aspect of the struggle: we have Corneille's conflict between passion and duty, the anarchist conflict between the individual and society, the Christian conflict between nature and grace. It is not part of our scheme to go deeply into the various forms of the conflict; we propose to confine ourselves to one: the dualism between life and spirit. And as both these terms have a certain ambiguity we must be careful to define them clearly at the outset. By life, we mean the sum total of those elements that connect man with the sensible universe: body, instincts, sensibility in all its forms. By spirit, we mean everything human that has its origin outside the Cosmos and is independent of its necessity: the intelligence and the will, with their train of implications—supersensible, and ultimately supernatural. The conflict we are going to discuss is simply the restraining of vital instincts by a moral law—taking the word "moral", here, in the very broad sense of the mind's control of conduct—and by a religious ideal.

Our point of view—and it is perhaps as well to emphasise the fact—will not be that of the metaphysician nor that of the theologian. In our observations and conclusions we shall no doubt encounter, from time to time, both metaphysics and theology, but we shall not be speaking in their name. Ours will be a concrete realm, that of human experience and the history of morals. What we are studying is not man in himself, nor is it the Christian in himself; it is man and the Christian as they have actually lived in the past, as they live now on this earth, with all their errors, stumblings and strivings, and that tragic interval between humanity and man, between the Christian and Christianity.

THE FRUITFULNESS OF THE CONFLICT

There is another fact that can scarcely be challenged: this conflict between life and spirit—a kind of flaw in man's vital perfection—contributes powerfully to the perfecting of his *humanity*. Nothing pure or great has ever flourished in this world without asceticism and without suffering. Only shallow hedonists, or those thinkers who have doubted either the existence or the positive value of the spirit, have considered as wholly bad this strain and tension that inhabits mankind. But the wisdom of all the ages, the wisdom of every people, has unanimously sanctified this inward anguish; and it is one of the glories of the human race that, against its universal repugnance to sacrifice, it has set its no less universal intuition that the function of sacrifice is something divine—

> To spirit adding what is reft from flesh.

In man—especially in the period of his youth—there is a certain exuberance, a thick and turbid ebullition of his vital powers, that has the effect of imprisoning and seducing the spirit: this must be overcome and transcended before man can be truly himself. Nourished and measured by the flesh and the senses, our earliest passions are limited and exclusive, impenetrable like the body itself from which they emanate; and it is through the vanquishing of these passions that there emerge at last, in all their richness and clarity, the sublimest examples of our thought and love. Out of how many passions, wrought upon by trials, comes that peace of heart associated with true love! All but the shallowest way of living involves the tearing up of one rough draft after another:

> Our earliest loves are love's probationing,
>> Brief transitory joys, a fitful flame
>> In souls imperfect, hearts confused by shame,
> Where stirs a short and vague awakening.
> To know love's heights, love undiminishing,
>> The heart must natural frailties disclaim,
>> Endure long toil, the pangs without a name,
> The forging blows and painful tempering.[1]

[1] Aug. Angellier, *A l'amie perdue.*

Man is born suffering into his life in time. But his birth into eternity involves still greater pangs. His all too sensible raptures are warm like flesh—and like flesh corruptible. Their furtive destiny is governed by the great law, that of absolute change and total oblivion. But this general cosmic acquiescence in death, translated into the human sphere, becomes faithlessness and ingratitude.

> On loves forsaken, children dead, I feed,
> On laughing widowhood and godless creed,
>   On all the black forgotten things;
> *All sensual pleasures are to me akin . . .*

Thus Victor Hugo's worm within the tomb. And it is true enough that the joys most sought-after are those that contain the seeds and very savour of death. It is possible to be resigned to this tragic affinity between rapture and annihilation; one may even hold, with Gide, that inconstancy and oblivion hold all the riches of humanity: "Haste, inconstant soul! Know that the fairest flower is the first to fade. Savour its fragrance quickly. The immortelle has none." But all the aphorisms of this philosophy of the transitory avail nothing to slake that thirst for secure happiness which is at the very core of our human nature. And Dante's great question—"How may man make himself eternal?"—re-echoes still in the hearts of all of us. There is only one answer: the fight against self, renunciation of self, war . . .

We can put aside, here, the theological problem of original sin. Psychologically, it is not difficult to verify the dogma of the fall—as did Jacques Rivière in his well-known study—with a thousand concrete and very cogent examples. However free one may be from dogmatic "prejudice", one has only to look at man as he is to be vaguely aware that here is a being who is not at home within himself, that he has somehow fallen below the level of his proper nature, that to regain the destiny that is rightfully his, however precariously and incompletely, he must be for ever climbing a difficult slope. In him, life and spirit are severed and opposed: life, instead of serving spirit, tends to enslave it; spirit, in order to escape the wiles of this Circe, often ceases to be the guide of life and becomes its tyrant.

But it is a sign of mental laziness to explain this human dualism by original sin alone. There is no occasion to abuse what is really a profound truth by making it behave as a fantastic *Deus ex machina*. All moral problems can be resolved eventually into ontological problems: a being that falls shows by its mere act of falling that its nature is such that it is liable to fall. It is safe to say that man in a pure state of nature (unaffected, that is, by either sin or miracle) would still be the victim of some inward tension. Here we have to deal with the whole question of human nature. A plant, or an animal, receives its whole nature (as it were) all at once; without external interference, it is inevitably what it must be. But man—and here is the essential mark that distinguishes him from all other beings, whether superior or inferior to himself—does not receive his humanity at the outset. It is only slowly and painfully that the spirit emerges; its development, both intellectual and emotional, depends very largely on its own choosing and striving. There is no merit in being a stone, an animal or an angel; but there is merit in being a man. All other beings simply are what they are: man *becomes* what he is. He must conquer his own nature. . . . But conquest means fighting. It is in human nature itself that the human conflict has its roots: sin has aggravated and polluted, but not wholly created it.

"If thy eye is an occasion for falling, pluck it out." What are these words of Christ but a recognition of this inner conflict?

THE VANITY OF THE CONFLICT

Conflict is necessary and fruitful because man is divided. But however deep-seated this inner dualism may be, it is none the less true that man is a unity, and that the conflict between spirit and life, when pushed too far and considered as something absolute, involves in a common ruin both spirit and life. Life and spirit in man are indissolubly compounded: a too violent preference for either is inhuman. . . .

"The spirit of God brooded over the waters." The spirit of man is borne upon the waters of his vitality: if the waters rise too high, the frail barque of the spirit may be swept away and destroyed; this is the danger that justifies asceticism, which has no other object in itself but to enable the spirit to navigate the waters of life. I use the word "asceticism" in the very broad sense of a firm control of sensuous life by the element of the spirit: from this point of view one could claim that asceticism is the foundation of all the major manifestations of human culture.

But canalising a stream is not the same as drying it up. The asceticism that becomes an end in itself—either through narrowness or routine—turns into a hatred of life, and in so doing reacts to the detriment of the spirit. The waters that wreck the vessel when they rise too high, when they fall too low run it aground in the sand. Indeed, one has only to look at the products of asceticism in some of its forms—whether it be an anaemic moralism or a desiccated intellectualism—to discover a striking resemblance to a ship run aground in a waste of sand.

At the root of many spiritual ideals there lies a deep misunderstanding of two essential character-istics of the life of the senses: complexity and change. Certain systems of morality look like dangerous encroachments by the pure idea—I was going to say the fixed idea, and it is perhaps not without reason that the *idée fixe* has acquired a derogatory sense in present-day language—encroachments on what should rightly be the domain of human life and action. They demand of man an impossible simpli-city, an immobility of nature; they crush the live becoming under a dead eternity: Stoic quietism, for example, or Corneille's morality of honour, or the nineteenth-century cult of respectability. Man,

under such systems, is no longer allowed to change;
he has not even the right to look about him as he
walks: it is not only a yoke he has to wear, but
blinkers as well! Everything in his mobile and multi-
farious life must be stifled by a static and cut-and-
dried principle. "His vows", says Racine, "take the
place of love." The spirit goes before—*the spirit is
willing enough.* . . . Life follows after as best it may—
or stays where it is! Moral systems of this sort merely
pervert the duty of loyalty; they contribute nothing
to that need for renewal and forgetting, a need that
is felt by every living being and helps to ensure an
element of freshness and originality. In congealing
life, the spirit congeals itself; the eternity that kills
becoming, instead of integrating it within itself, is
not that living eternity which nourishes time; it is
nothing but a phantom, a mere abstraction.

But there is something worse than the spirit's
oppression and mechanising of life—which recoils on
the spirit and is bound to formalise it—and that is
the falsifying of spiritual values, the contaminating
of the spirit by stemming up the natural energies
of life. Morals and ideals, which deny their legiti-
mate rights to the body and the individual, not only
wear down life, they contrive to pervert it. Life, thus
suppressed, does not fade out of sight, nor is it transformed into spirit; what it does is to proceed to
dissemble with the spirit: posing as spirit itself, it
reappears surreptitiously in the guise of "higher"
values. Moralists of every age have denounced this
counterfeit; they might well see here a result of

man's unhappy state. What I see is the fruit of his overweening ambitions. No one becomes a forger for the simple reason that he is poor, but because, being poor, he wants to become rich. There are, or have been, social and affective climates that repress, and reduce to the status of the "shameful", elemental feelings like the sexual instinct or a simple zest for life; such feelings, we may well conceive, indestructible as they are and deprived of their normal outlet, must strive to attain their ends by dressing themselves up in the ideal that condemns them! In a moral atmosphere that allowed scope to no other sentiment but that of patriotism, one of Corneille's heroines, learning that the man she loves is about to marry the queen, accounts for her involuntary sigh at hearing the news by declaring:

> To see the sceptre in so young a hand
> I sighed in pity for my native land.

Her father, with some subtlety, corrects her "perverse" adaptation of passion to ideal, of life to spirit:

> The public interest rarely draws a sigh
> Unless some grudge with martyrdom ally:
> Both, hiding one another, falsely prate;
> At thy age none commiserates the State.

There is no need to support our contention by quoting angelically pure ideals, all compounded with libido, or those political myths, founded ostensibly on the purest spirit of collectivism, but in fact the worst kind of selfish individualism. This spontaneous hypocrisy, this cynical prostitution of the spirit and its noblest values, is a blot on romanticism in all its forms. Romanticism, whether artistic, political or religious, is always a morbid confusion of the vital with the spiritual, of the things of the world with the things of heaven; and the confusion is always cloaked with some lofty ideal. According to Goethe it is romanticism itself that is unhealthy. But the romantic lie is not generated spontaneously; its coming is invariably prepared by a false idea of the relations between spirit and life, either by a false asceticism or a false classicism. Behind Rousseauist putrefaction stands the inhuman rigidity of Calvin. . . . There lie the mistakes of all exaggerated spiritualisms. The pretence of stemming or neglecting the elements of healthy life renders life itself sickly, and this sickly life corrupts and enslaves the spirit. Ideals too lofty to take account of the world and the flesh presently degenerate into pretexts, for the world and the flesh to use freely for their own ends. The spirit is never so nearly the slave of life as when it sets itself up to be the tyrant of life.

There is no doubt, however, that the cults and moralities that overstress spiritual values, conferring on them an almost autonomous privilege, by so doing encourage the interior life. True, the things of the spirit are in fact, and in the deepest sense, far superior to the things of life: it is a higher and truer calling to be a great poet than a good workman; the vocation of a nun who consecrates herself to God is something higher than the vocation of the best of mothers. But the values of life have this important advantage: they are *sincere*. It is hardly possible for a normal person to entertain any illusions (or transfer them to others) about his own physical strength or personal dexterity: here the criteria of worth are far too exact and easy to check! It is not the same with spiritual values: these being immaterial, and belonging so much to the invisible world, contrive to evade all precise control and, very often, all objective control. A bad poet may persuade himself he is a genius unappreciated, but no weakling can pretend to be an unrecognised giant! The more exalted a human activity, the more difficult it is to "know it by its fruits", these being so mysterious and remote. . . . But difficulty of control is an invitation to fraud. The bitter tragedy of the highest human values lies precisely in the fact that they are so easily counterfeited. How is one to judge—if it be not with the aid of a rare and penetrating wisdom, the reaction of time and always challengeable fashion—the genuineness of a political or artistic vocation, or for that matter the genuineness of a religious vocation? Besides, it is only natural that many of those whose impotence or mediocrity would be obvious in ordinary social activities should seek compensation by devoting themselves to the service of "higher ideals": their inferiority, here, cannot be directly confirmed; they may even succeed, if they have the knack of expressing what they are unable to experience, in obtaining a brilliant if transitory success. An indifferent carpenter will never thrive at his trade, but an incompetent politician and a bogus mystic may throw enough dust into the eyes of the public to secure for themselves a resounding triumph. We see it happening all too obviously every day. It is normal, too, with man—for whom spiritual realities are not the object of direct intuition but are merely apprehensible through the medium of the senses—that the noblest values are also those that are most vulnerable to humbug. That is one of the many weaknesses of the *incarnate* spirit: it has given rise, side by side with counterfeited ideals, to a host of "debunkers", who react so strongly against spiritual sham as to challenge the worth and the very existence of spiritual values.

But the life-spirit dualism does not necessarily tend to the advantage of the spirit. It also happens—and the two errors correspond just as day to night—that man may decide in favour of life instead of spirit. The myths of a total return to life or to nature have flourished in all ages, and in none more than ours. It is one of man's oldest dreams to shed his obligations, his ideals and promises, and abandon himself thoroughly to a good cosmic existence. This would seem to be the central theme of much contemporary literature. Also, the law of the unity and interdependence of spirit and life still operates. To play the animal succeeds no better than to play the angel; because in fact we are men. The autarchic pretensions of vital values are bound to end miserably in the *falsifying* of vital values. The spirit, which it is sought to eliminate in the name of life, steals back into the heart of life and poisons it. Those who would decapitate man only succeed in driving his head into his bowels, and making him think with his bowels. Examine carefully the life of those enemies of the spirit, enemies of moral and intellectual values, and you will see what is the secret motive of their revolt: not life in its animal simplicity, but still spirit—a furtive and disguised spirit, searching for itself by way of the flesh and the senses. The revolt of life against spirit becomes the revolt of spirit against itself. Disgusted by a false asceticism, the spirit turns its craving for mastery and knowledge upon the things of the senses: it plays the card of life! How many desire the forbidden fruit, not because it is sweet (a perfectly healthy biological reason), but merely because it is forbidden! Their sins are not due to vital attraction but spiritual curiosity. They themselves are not indifferent, as they would have us believe, to all considerations of morals or logic; under the cloak of life, or nature or pleasure, they construct a counter-logic and a counter-morality of their own. They are more conventional in their revolt than the conventions they attack. What could possibly be tamer or more banal than their whims, less fantastic than their fantasies? They are conventionally spontaneous, artificially natural. Their final disguise is to go naked. Freud, to quote only one example, whose pansexualism is simply a theoretical expression of the sex-hypertrophy of the modern man, has never described the sexual instinct as such: the sexuality by which man, according to him, is wholly governed, is derived from a sneaking and debased form of logic; Prinzhorn was justified in seeing in his work an elaborate attempt to rationalise the instinct.

Thus the conflict, left to itself, produces shams and obscenities. Spirit and life were intended to be *united and distinct*. To separate them is to confound them. Unity, betrayed, revenges itself by confusion: the flesh, driven to earth, emerges once more wearing the mask of the spirit; the spirit, banished, reappears in the guise of life.

There is a sentence in the Gospel that we may interpret as the condemning of all these vain contests between the spirit and life: "What God has joined, let not man put asunder."

THE ROOT OF THE CONFLICT: IDOLATRY

From whatever standpoint one regards man in the concrete, the thing that strikes one first is this: here is a creature who is fundamentally incomplete; nothing can wholly satisfy him; he wanders vainly in quest of fulfilment.

One may believe that this tension, this insufficiency, is without remedy, that it is part and parcel of human nature: man is merely a great desire, yawning to the void; he is condemned by nature to feed upon his own hunger, he can never be perfectly fulfilled. Such has been the conclusion of all those thinkers, from Heraclitus to Nietzsche and Freud, who have been unable to comprehend how there can be unity in division, God in man, and so have ended by deifying war. But it is also conceivable that this sterile conflict within man is accidental. Exercising this strange primacy of his, endowed as he is with reason, man could not, unlike every other being in the world, be a question without an answer. His full completion exists, but in some mysterious manner he is deprived of it. Thus we return to the doctrine of original sin, that is—taking the word in its most metaphysical sense—to the rupture between man and his final destiny.

We who are Christians know that the completion man craves, he lost at the very beginning. The essence of original sin lies in the withdrawal of man within himself, in his rupture with God. It is a trite and overworked expression, "to break with God". Let us be rid, for a moment, of abstraction and verbalism, and take the word God in what one might call its personal and affective sense: God is the thing that fulfils and satisfies, the reality in which man can develop and find perfect repose. Anyone who is not aware of a lively feeling of security and supreme achievement, even in the direst sufferings, is more or less separated from God, separated from his end, and thus inwardly divided. He who declines any master but himself is not his own master. Man's end, in fact, is one with his nature: it is impossible to suppress the one without destroying the other. How should a being who is not one with his origin be one with himself? As well expect a plant, deprived of

water and light, to succeed in achieving its vegetal
destiny! Separation from God results inevitably in
an interior separation: man is at war with himself
because he is alone with himself.

The way the conflict is generated is easy to follow.
Rupture with God does not end the need for God,
the craving to be in communion with something
ultimate and sustaining. It is thus that isolation
begets idolatry. In the man separated from God,
everything in turn is called upon to become God.
It is a terrible curse upon the children of Adam that
everything they love must usurp the qualities of the
absolute. Wherever they look, it is their completion
they seek, and the moment they desire a thing they
must turn it into an idol.

But it is the nature of idols to be exclusive. Their
appetites, to use a fashionable term, are totalitarian.
Everything that is not themselves they repudiate.
Hence the conflict. . . . The thing that starts the
quarrel between spirit and life—the two entities that
divide human life between them—is what is at once
most universal and most central. Its ramifications
can be seen in countless sub-conflicts, for every part
of man, every aspect, can become an idol. Without
leaving our own age we have examples in the *homo
sexualis* of Freud and the *homo politicus* of Mussolini,
in the *homo ethnicus* of Hitler and the *homo oeconomicus*
of Marx—each an idolatrous and bloated enlarge-
ment of one side of man, and each in conflict with
all the rest that it seeks to obliterate or absorb. And
the conflicts are unappeasable, because the antagonists

are not human realities: they are substitutes for God—in other words, they are idols.

It is also the nature of idols to deceive. None carries out the promises it makes, or rather what man makes it promise—and for the best of all reasons! Hence their multiplication and rapid succession; hence that passing—apparently so senseless, yet fundamentally so logical—"from one extreme to the other", an all but constant phenomenon in the history of men and morals. The succession of idols, and their conflict, is a symptom of the fidelity of man to his idolatry, of his constancy in isolation. "It is customary", as I wrote elsewhere, "to see human excesses simply as reactions against previous and opposite excesses." This view is not mistaken but it is somewhat elliptical. Basically, the opposed excesses that succeed one another are only two episodes in a single war against unity, and (we may as well say it) against God. It is true that idols hate each other, but their mutual hatred is only the reflection of a hatred they have in common. . . . Idols are only apparently in conflict; deep down they are all of them allied against God.

The impossibility, inherent in fallen man until he is restored by grace, of striking a harmonious balance between the various parts and functions of his being is very evident historically in the incredible fragility of every "classicism". This phenomenon, I think, has never been given the attention it deserves: every classical form by means of which man has tried, without having recourse to God, to realise order and harmony in himself—this was so in the age of Pericles and in the age of Virgil, in the Italian Renaissance and, to a large extent, in seventeenth-century France—every such form, which by reason of its apparent balance seemed destined for long duration, has actually passed like a flash, to give place to fresh anarchy and ever-renewed conflicts. Order is the exception in this world, disorder the rule; hence the factitious character of every humanism founded on man: the classical periods were like short and precarious truces in the course of a single unappeasable war. Only one classicism—I take the word to cover any doctrine or state of mind that aims to harmonise and unify the many vocations of man—has so far resisted time: and that is the Catholic Church. But it is only the body of the Church that is human!

In reality, then, it is not a question of conflict between spirit and life, but rather of a series of encounters between idols. Whether man, isolated from his true origin, makes intellect or will the object of his worship, or whether, disillusioned by spirit, he makes a complete return to earth and senses, what he keeps on craving for with every part of him is God. The life and spirit in him are related and complementary: it is not these that are mutually exclusive, it is the phantoms that are at war, the ghosts of the absolute. The tragedy lies in the fact that the scene of these ghostly battles is precisely the place that is *empty* of the true absolute.

GRACE VERSUS CONFLICT

It might at first appear daring to offer Christianity as a remedy for human conflict. In antiquity, it could be objected, surely man enjoyed a plenitude and an inner harmony far greater than anything known by the Christianised man? And did not Christ come, as he said himself, to bring a sword into the world, to kindle a fire—in other words, to stir up conflict?

The paradox can be resolved. Note, in the first place, that a certain neo-paganism, a very superficial and gullible neo-paganism, has greatly exaggerated this inner harmony of man in antiquity. Those Greeks, steeped (we are told) in order and wisdom, in whom flesh and spirit developed with equal energy, whose life flowed by like a tranquil river—they are all a figment of the donnish imagination. Antique man was devoted to idols, and therefore to conflict. We will put aside the humanism of a philosopher like Aristotle—a speculative rather than an actually experienced humanism—and pass in review some of the products of ancient culture and morals. What was, for example, the "ideal" man of Plato, or the Stoical will-man, or the collective man of Sparta and primitive Rome, not to mention the pre-Socratic man at grips with blind fates, or the *homo animalis* of St Paul—what were these, you may ask, but beings withdrawn into a mere part of themselves, in conflict with all the rest? We may grant, of course—and here is the half-truth, the origin of

those literary fictions about the harmony of soul
enjoyed by antiquity—the idolatry of the ancients
was far richer, very much healthier, than the idolatry
of the moderns. The ancients, like us, were at war
with their nature, but they experienced in their
fighting a kind of zest and stability, a security no
longer known to us now. Their conflicts might be
exhausting and poisonous ultimately, but not so
immediately as those of today: the deep foundations
of their vitality had not been corrupted by sin;
consequently nature, still fed by healthy reserves,
could better support follies and excesses than it can
today. The ancients achieved the paradox of putting
the maximum of humanity into situations that in
themselves were essentially inhuman. Life and
spirit could engage in a fight to the death without
suffering mutual exhaustion in the process. (Incidentally, this extraordinary capacity for conflict has
been continued—not to say developed—in Christianised humanity: one has only to take a glance at the
history of asceticism!) Today such a fearful ordeal
would spell total ruin. Without very rich resources,
interior division cannot be sustained with impunity.
Tomorrow we shall be indivisible—through sheer
exhaustion! Some return to unity is a vital necessity.
The time is not far distant when life and spirit, I
think, will be faced with an enforced symbiosis—
the enforced symbiosis of the blind and paralytic. . . .
God is spirit. And Christianity is a religion of the
spirit. But the spiritual fulfilment that Christianity
brings to man cannot be a fulfilment opposed to

life: grace assumes and "contains" life, because it comes from the Creator of Life. The Incarnation of the Word—the descent of pure and absolute spirit into the heart of the sensible world—bears powerful witness to this proximity, to this unity of spirit with vital realities, that is one of the essential marks of Christian truth.

In removing man from idols, grace also tends to remove him from conflicts. Union with God is bound to be achieved in a condition of inner harmony. No partial salvation could be sufficient for man: the resurrection of the body is a dogma that follows necessarily from the immortality of the soul.

It is easy enough to challenge this theory. In practice, Christianity seems to have brought the most violent conflicts into human life. The history of Christian asceticism is terrifying; in every age Christian morality, by anathematising the senses and the passions, seems to have striven to suppress and disparage life. It was in view of these considerations that thinkers like Nietzsche and Klages saw Christianity as "a work of death", an instrument for the mutilating of human nature, or for poisoning it beyond recovery.

In our view, the problem of "Christian conflict" has more than one meaning: it can be regarded under several very different aspects.

There is a condition of inner privation and tension, so it would seem, that makes for the germinating and developing of *affective* Christianity. It is here we meet the problem of the *anima naturaliter Christiana*.

Its data and solution vary widely with times and personalities. We are not concerned to deny that biospiritual balance and fulfilment may offer in itself—it often does—a fruitful ground for the manifestations of grace. But it is also undeniable that in fallen man (in man, that is, devoted to idols, deprived of the spontaneous knowledge and love of God) too much worldly harmony and assurance have often a blunting or isolating effect in regard to any appeal of the divine. If we consider the temperaments of men like St Augustine and Pascal, Baudelaire and Dostoevsky—I select these four, so different in character, because of the trait common to them all: a sensitiveness of heart and spirit to Christian values and especially to the central notions of sin and redemption—deep down in all of them we find a profound interior anguish. This conflict that "predisposes" to Christianity is not exactly that between spirit and life, it is something deeper still: a feeling of insecurity, of the insufficiency of nature when left to itself, the impossibility of relying fully on the things of earth and time, the tortured longing for an absolute reality, at once absent and present. . . . How many hearts are opened to grace because nature is closed to them! In falling below their own level they take their first step towards God. "The publicans and harlots are farther on the road to God's kingdom than you." It was to social outcasts that these words were meant to refer; but they can be applied, in a certain sense, to psychological outcasts. It would certainly be an exaggeration to accept, as a definition of a man predestined, that formulated by a certain hero of drama: "You to whom idols are most alluring and most vain; you whom the world most attracts and deceives; you who, wherever God is not, find death!" Yet it remains none the less true that the wounds inflicted on the soul by frustration and conflict may serve, in some cases, to give admittance to grace. This concrete and purely accidental fact was enlarged by Nietzsche into a general rule, a law capable of explaining everything. Christianity, he proclaimed boldly, is essentially the product of vital degeneracy and interior conflict; the Christian, according to him, is simply a "sick animal". . . .

Apart altogether from this conflict, that may be said to be "preparatory" to Christianity, there is also a pseudo-Christian conflict between spirit and life. History has a lot to teach us about this. Many Christian ascetics and ascetical writers have persecuted vital values, the things of the earth and the senses, with an intransigence incompatible with the very nature of Christianity. They give the impression of seeking the supreme goal of man in the crushing of life rather in union with God, or at any rate of making a deadly conflict between life and spirit the necessary condition of union with God. Alas, Christ's message is one thing, the use men make of it another: much idolatry can flourish in a Christian conscience, many idols can be mistaken for the Christian God. . . . When erected into a doctrine, hatred of life and the sensible world has been condemned by the Church as heretical. But apart from doctrinal heresy, there has been a very prolific emotional heresy; and innumerable souls, faithful to the Church intellectually, have guided their feelings and actions by a sort of practical Manicheism. The sight of certain ascetics, concentrating all their energy upon a hopeless inner struggle, makes one wonder with good reason whether they have ever known the *Other* and the deliverance brought by love, or whether, tragically self-enclosed, they are not simply sacrificing their lower to their higher self. Yet it is as well, here, to be on one's guard against summary and premature judgements: the Church is an organic body in time and space, and each of its elements can be appreciated only in its functional relation to the whole. Errors like exaggerated asceticism, deprived—at any rate in this world—of individual finality, may be preparing the way for profounder harmonies to come, to still newer mysteries; hence they may possess a kind of historical and collective finality. Even those who stray may help the progress of the convoy—if only by indicating where the true way lies! What St Paul had to say about the necessity of heresies is even truer, surely, of emotional heresies than heresies of theory.

Finally there is the true and healthy Christian conflict. This is destructive of nothing but what is negative; it is mortal only to death. It sets in opposition, not two things that are complementary, but two things mutually exclusive in themselves: not life and spirit, but the old self-enclosed man and the new man open to God. Grace is at war with all idols, whether these call themselves life (the anarchy of the senses) or spirit (a haughty rationalism or an exaltation of the will); and we have seen already that this dualism is vain and that every idol is at once life and spirit, having its birth, previous to any interior schism, in the original divorce of man from God. It is the work of grace to break this isolation: the war to which it gives rise in us is the only war that has its basis in love; it is no longer the hopeless war of the ego against itself, but a war of liberation, that of the Other and the self. And the victory of Love, by reconciling man with that Other who is also his deepest self (*interior intimo meo*, in the words of St Augustine) reconciles man with himself. The Christian conflict is the struggle of the whole against the revolted part, it is therefore a war on war. It is a combat that none the less, if it is to be crowned with success, is often fought at the cost of intensest agony, for war and falsehood are so deeply ingrained in us as to usurp the appearance of peace and health. The Christian conflict is essentially liberating: its end is the unity and deliverance of man.

Christianity makes an end of both the spirit-idol and the life-idol, in conflict as these are, yet at the same time intermingled. It teaches the soul the separate but converging paths of what are truly spirit and life; it gives life to the things of the spirit and it spiritualises the things of life.

The Christian spirit is itself also life. It is instructive to note how, in every age and among all peoples, there has been a shrewd idea that a kind of antinomy

exists between living according to the spirit (in
conformity, that is, with reason and morals) and just
living. The prejudice appears in a number of popular
phrases, like "living one's life", "leading a life", and
so on. The last formula is very curious: if it is
"leading a life" to reject all rules of the spirit and
surrender to vice, what do the virtuous do? Lead a
death, presumably. The implication is intriguing.
And there are certain grounds for it. Man is deeply
embedded in the material creation, summing up
within himself all its various stages; but he partici-
pates very feebly in the things of the spirit. It is
therefore only to be expected that for man, and *a
fortiori* for man isolated from God, the things of the
spirit should seem colourless and unnatural, somehow akin to death. Constraint is necessary to live by
an ethical principle, even to learn how to read; but it
involves no arduous learning merely to see or to feel!
The spirit, in this world, lacks life because it lacks
maturity. But the maturity of the spirit is the love of
the spirit. The spirit can live only when it loves. And
it can never truly love except in a Christian climate.
Bereft of grace, what is called spiritual love looks
like something very different: a kind of collusion, a
collusion between an intellectual pose and an in-
toxication of the senses. Its very fragility clearly
indicates a lack of true spiritual roots. Christianity
alone gives man the love of the spirit as such. He who
has never known that universal overflowing—that
intimate communion with the immaterial, love's
sovereign independence of all sensible and individual

contingencies—knows nothing of that *tenderness of the spirit* which is the essence of Christianity. In a saint, the life of the spirit is something warm and immediate like a sensation, virtue is spontaneous, "natural"; the law, fed almost biologically by blood and sap, is a flower to be inhaled, an intoxicating draught.[1] The life of the spirit cannot possibly hate "life". Christian love is a spiritual love, but a love *incarnate*. It enters into the flesh and the senses, not to suppress them, but to imbue them fully with its own purity. It is not from life that it draws its essential plenitude, but from God; yet in that plenitude it associates life. Two scriptural expressions illustrate this perfect unity of life and spirit, a thing impossible to man and possible only to God: *God is spirit*, and *God is love*.

But what is truly flesh is also, in one sense, spirit. There are two ways in which human sensibility may impede the spirit. The first has to do with the excessive exuberance of a too full-blooded vitality (this is the case with primitives and with the young, driven blindly hither and thither by the gusts of passion). The second is just the opposite: it is due to the enfeebling of the vital powers when, deprived of their natural development, they morbidly ape the spirit and encroach on its domain. It has been said very wisely that "the flesh that denies God (the flesh, that is, which declines to obey the laws of the spirit) is unhealthy flesh, a flesh of morbid dreams". Life, in both cases, is false to its true and *human* dimension. Man's instincts and passions are made for the spirit:

[1] Cf. Psalm 118.

in their normal condition they are open and receptive to that immaterial force which is their completion and also their crowning glory. But it is only the divine spirit that is rich enough, strong enough, to control and crown life and restore it to its true destiny. On the one hand, it moderates the anarchic violence of the passions, still enveloped in animalism; on the other—and in our age of vital exhaustion it is here that its influence is most beneficial and necessary—by leading man to his true spiritual fulfilment, it renders useless and dispenses with both spiritual mimicry and vitiated sensibility, it buries the phantoms of the imagination beneath a reality that is sweeter and lovelier than all dreams; thereby it heals the flesh and restores it to its normal function, which is not to play at being spirit, but to be in communion with the spirit whilst remaining what it is. *Et omnia adjicientur vobis.* He who first seeks spiritual health receives in addition animal health, and it is through recovering the angel we find we are in possession of the healthy animal.

But there are two ways in which this unity, the normal goal of the Christian conflict, may be missed. In other words, the Christian conflict is liable to a double check.

There exists first of all—we have already stressed this point—an exaggerated asceticism which, instead of aiming at the *transfiguring* of life, is bent on *disfiguring* it. Certain ascetics seem doomed to save but a fraction of themselves; they turn their backs on unity and deify conflict. There is something grim about this ascetic instinct that functions apart from the direct service of love; what actuates the vine-presser is not the expectation of wine but an insensate zest for destruction; death, that in normal asceticism is the mere servant of a higher life, seems almost as though it were to be given a free reign. But side by side with this asceticism, that would put an impass-able barrier between life and spirit, we may see a tendency no less dangerous to unite them too quickly, and at too low a level. Quietism (a word that, for me, has more than a theological meaning) is seeking to realise a synthesis of life and spirit, of nature and grace, before man has attained to a sufficient degree of purification. The result is not unity, but the mutual falsification of vital and spiritual values. This false peace is even more unhealthy than the worship of war. False asceticism, moreover, has a fatal tendency to engender quietism: corpse-like rigidity is necessarily followed by putrefaction. Obviously, the fighter is never so near to giving up, and tamely acquiescing in a peace without victory, as when he concludes that the struggle is hopeless. He who sees the flesh as intrinsically evil, stubbornly rebellious against the spirit, has only to relax his ascetic tension very momentarily and he will suc-cumb most grossly and miserably to the flesh: his dualist conception of the nature of man precludes in advance any attempt to synthesise or transfigure it. Hence the statism and inertia of the quietists. Whether it results, as with the Greek cynics or the Manicheans, in a display of brutal sensuality or, as with the Christian quietists of modern times, in sly manifestations of debased vitality disguised by a mask of religious virtues (humility, simplicity, resignation), false asceticism in both cases bears a common fruit: man is dispensed from the spiritual integration of his instincts; for the unity of life and spirit there is substituted their co-existence and confusion. He who would be wholly angel will end as grossly animal: he has been too prone to consider the animal in him a stranger, he has driven it too far from his centre, to be able to tame it any more or raise it to a higher level. History, showing the close and regular con-nection between false asceticism and quietist reaction provides all we need to confirm this theory.

If we may now take a general view of the Catholic spirituality of today and tomorrow, we notice first —and this observation is by no means new—that it bears witness to a "broadening of the ways of the Lord", a descent of the sacred into the profane, of the eternal into the temporal, of the spirit into life, to an extent that has never been known hitherto. There is a psychological as well as a social side to this movement: on the one hand, grace tends more and more to impregnate and exalt the natural and vital values; on the other, affective and even mystical Christianity is progressively spreading among the laity, among those whose vocations are temporal. The things of the earth and the flesh, recognised at last and adopted by the spirit, need no longer be hidden in darkness or issue forth disguised; passions and instincts (and here I am thinking specially of the

sexual instinct, which has given birth in the past to
so many inhibitions and misconceptions) can find
simultaneous scope in their biological integrity and
in full communion with spiritual love. It would seem
that, amid the ruins of the modern soul, a new unity
is seeking the light. The regard of the spirit, the
benediction of the spirit, is reaching down into the
nethermost depths of nature; man in his entirety is
being restored to God. Already a sense of the sacred,
a mystical influence and awe, is forming a kind of
halo about the most mundane realities. Catholic
sanctity, of course, was always profoundly human,
but there is no denying that in most of the saints of
past ages there was an exaggerated tension between
the vital and the spiritual, a certain incapacity to
unify the plenitude of the divine with the normal
exercise of biological faculties, especially with the
vocation of marriage. There will arise tomorrow,
perhaps, a new type of sanctity, in which lovers of
God will be completely human. . . .

But we must take care not to separate the present
from the past. This new form of spirituality that
seems to be arising today is the fruit of all the anguish
and all the strivings that have gone before. I have
always thought (but this is a theme that needs
developing at length and can be only briefly indicated here) that the human development of Christianity has involved not only those "nights", described by the mystics for purifying divine love in
individuals, but "historical nights", vast trials in the
upward progress of humanity during which new ages

of spirituality are prepared. The first Christian generation, intoxicated by the actual *image* of Christ, by the echo of his voice and the immediate expectation of the end of the world, knew what corresponds to the sensible fulfilment of beginners. Then came the night of the senses, the withdrawing of love into the spirit. But at least the spirit—and this continued throughout the Middle Ages—was firmly and healthily attached to God. Finally, from the Renaissance onwards, there descended upon the Christian world the night of the spirit.

Whatever truth there may be in this theory, if we try to compare, in the matter of the relations between life and spirit, the Christian spirituality of yesterday with that which is likely to emerge tomorrow, we seem to observe the following evolution. The ascetic's retreat, his flight from life and realities, is in process of being transformed; exceptional conditions of existence, a complete forgoing of certain natural faculties, are conditions, not useless, but less and less *necessary* to deep communion with God and to the steeping of the soul in charity. A saint can be a perfectly normal person: I mean, by that, he need not be in the least superhuman. Humanity is tending today to eliminate, not only what is left of the anti-natural prejudice, but also that element of physical heroism which went so often with the sanctity of the past. Of course, there are two reasons for this: a deeper consciousness both of God and ourselves which preserves us at the outset from certain confusions; and, secondly, an appreciable exhaustion of vitality which no longer permits great ascetic exertions. At any rate, the association of the superhuman with the supernatural is coming to an end.[1] Thérèse of Lisieux—the cloistered nun whose influence is felt in every stratum of the lay world—seems just at the moment to be forming a bridge between these two "styles" of sanctity we have been describing. It would seem quite likely that, in the history of Christian spirituality, her doctrine will have a rôle rather analogous to that of St Benedict at the close of antiquity.

This new spirituality, by the very fact of its being more open, more welcoming to nature and the senses, is also essentially much more independent of nature and the senses, much more free from excessive preoccupation with the flesh. The birth of unity means the death of confusion. He who ignores the life of the senses, or stems it up within himself, encourages it to assume some divine disguise, to seek insidious gratification under cover of a dubious impulse of the

---

[1] I forbear to pass judgement here on the value of these different forms of spirituality. Their essence, after all, is one. The same God dwells in the souls of all the saints, but in different modes. All we would say is that sanctity is tending to be more human and universal. Not that this implies any watering-down. Asceticism and the Cross will never be absent from Christian life in its higher forms; but heroism and sacrifice, instead of being finally realised in any superhuman fashion, will gradually make their way into the framework of ordinary daily life. This is the "fidelity in little things" preached by Thérèse of Lisieux. There is even reason to think that in this way the folly of the Cross, so far from being eliminated, will be infused ever more deeply into human life and action. The more a man is open to himself and to the world, the more open he is to its joys; true, but if he is ready to consecrate these joys to supreme love, the more open he is also to the Cross.

spirit. This is the origin of those unpleasant perversions of sensuality and spirit so frequently denounced by ascetical writers. But he who faces up squarely to his whole nature, above all he who sees the things of earth in their specific reality, can no longer confound within himself the earthly with the heavenly. However little he gives to God, he will not pay it in false coin. The less the spirit plays the tyrant to life, the less it is in danger of finding itself its dupe.[1]

In the Catholic world today there is a powerful intellectual movement on foot which aims at spiritualising the things of the body and of life. The hour has come to rehabilitate nature. . . . And it is only just that it should be so. But we should be on our guard, in this connection, against possible misapprehensions. Talking about a synthesis of grace and nature is not the same as realising it in one's life. There are certain apostles of the spirituality of nature who, through the very fact of their religious vocation, are lacking in the necessary personal experience. In natures that are in any way cramped and self-enclosed, living apart from some of the realities of the flesh leads to looking with something like horror at these realities; at the same time, in open and generous

---

[1] These remarks, of course, should not be taken to impugn the dignity (and in certain cases the necessity) of abstention in the exercise of certain vital powers, and especially of the sexual life. Here absolute sacrifice (clerical and religious celibacy) will always be a powerful means of union with God. Married life in union with God also implies sacrifice and struggle. But in both cases, I think, this struggle is more and more tending (and it is all to the good) to take place in perfect simplicity and openness, without the element of false-absolute and false-mystery that used to weigh so heavily on it in the past.

souls it gives rise to many illusions about the purity of the flesh and the degree to which it may be permeated by the spirit. Those who have known the depths of unhappy human nature know its rich capabilities and its mysterious intimacy with the soul and with God; but these are no less aware of its opacity, of its inertia and power of resistance to the spirit. However strong their sense of unity, they can never be blind to the terrible dualism that gnaws at the soul of man. It is a noble and beneficent ideal to preach to youth, that of the harmonious absorption of the flesh by the spirit, of becoming by eternity; but the doctrine is never quite healthy without a simultaneous warning of how slippery are life's paths, of what the passion of today can make of yesterday's vows, and of how tomorrow, perhaps, the eternal may have a baleful resemblance to death. Such warnings must be given of the struggle that is necessary to defend the ideal. There is a danger, otherwise, of producing a generation of mere utopians, to be succeeded by another that is wholly spoilt, a generation without faith in anything at all. The perfect union of flesh and spirit is not a flower to be picked for the stooping, and it must not be represented as such; but as a *stella rectrix* to which we must guide our steps without perilous dallying in deceptions and shadows. Too many have sought to extinguish that star they were given as a guide, and so have denied their ideal and lost their own souls.

Man, it is clear, will never have done with conflict. The thing to be condemned, to be liquidated as soon as may be, is not asceticism itself, it is the idolatry of asceticism.

"The secret of a happy and contented life", wrote Pascal, "is to avoid being at war with God or with nature." There was the true Pascal: a Pascal transcending and condemning Jansenism, a Pascal in perfect agreement with St Thomas. The double "peace" that Pascal preaches is indivisible. Whoever is not at peace with nature cannot be wholly at peace with God, for God is the author of nature, and nature is a vehicle of grace. Similarly, whoever is at war with God cannot be at peace with nature, for nature is no isolated and autonomous reality but a vessel in which the waters of the divine are received, a solicitation to grace. Grace needs nature and nature needs grace. The opposing of one to the other is the cleaving in two of God. God's *image* which is nature, and his *reality* which is grace, are meant to be united in one and the same love.

The true conflict, as we have seen, is not between life and spirit; it is between yes and no, communion and isolation, God and idol. And the conflict is resolved not by deciding between spirit and life, each of which is but a part of man, but in choosing the love that is the whole of man. In this love, life and spirit, grace and nature, are once and for all united. He whose love for God does not include God's work does not really love God; and he whose love for nature does not include God has no love for nature. All love that is fully itself—that is, fully mature—is in union with the love that is divine.

Admittedly it has been said: "If thy eye is an occasion for falling . . ." But the eye here means the idol—separation and withdrawal—so that the plucking it out is still the same struggle not to "put asunder what God has joined". This it is that reconciles two principles in the Gospel that are apparently opposed: love and its unity embraces everything in man—even conflict. Christ did not come into the world to destroy war, he came to make war serve the purposes of peace.

CHAPTER II

Sense and Spirit

WHAT is feeling—that part of our affective life that is immersed in the flesh and intrinsically dependent on it? We feel as the animals do, said a Father of the Church; but we think with the angels. The remark is ambiguous. Neither the animal life nor the spiritual exists in us in a pure state. Our feeling is that of a spiritual being, our mind is that of a sensuous being; the deepest law of our nature lowers our spirit towards the flesh, but at the same time it exalts the flesh towards the spirit. This ontological law is convincingly verified in the domain of action. Strictly speaking, we are aware of neither sensuous nor spiritual activities, but only *human* activities. The most brutish actions of the flesh (the act of eating, for example) implies a certain consent and delectation of the mind; conversely, the loftiest spiritual activity is dependent on a minimum of sensuous co-operation. Even the night of the senses is something "sensed". There is an experience of absence. Psychologically all we can state about the matter is this: no human act, whether of the senses or of the mind, is performed in complete isolation; but among these human acts, all of them compounded of feeling and spirit, some are inclined and polarised towards the senses, others towards the spirit.

THE ANTAGONISM

The most fundamental of our interior experiences shows two realities in apparent contradiction: the mysterious unity of feeling and spirit, with the inseparable synthesis of all their manifestations, and on the other hand their mutual antagonism. From the individual and collective history of mankind we learn how the freedom, power and purity of the spirit cost a bitter discipline of the life of the senses. Human greatness is inseparable from asceticism. More than any other ideal of wisdom or heroism, Christianity, seeking the growth of the spiritual life into the divine, accentuates this antagonism between the soul and the flesh, between the old unregenerate man and the new. It is with good reason that the history of Christianity, to an idolatrous apostle of "life" like Nietzsche, seems a vast crucifixion of all the delights and loves of the senses. The teachings of many Christian ascetics and teachers, taken as a basis for speculation, readily lend themselves to a dualist interpretation of human nature.[1] In fact, we have become so used to this paradox that we tend to be blind to its deeper meaning. Fundamentally there is something baffling in this conflict at the very heart of an absolute solidarity. How can there be so radical

[1] Many religious heresies and philosophical aberrations proceed from the fact that their authors, theoretically at any rate, have never surmounted the difficulty of human conflict. Those who took sides with the spirit saw the world of the senses as obscene and demon-ridden (e.g. the Manicheans and other heretics); those who sided with the senses treated the spirit as a "parasite of life" (Freud, for instance, and in a finer and deeper sense, Nietzsche and Klages).

an antagonism between two forces that are really inseparable, interdependent and substantially one?

Some put the blame upon original sin. Far be it from us to extenuate its misdeeds! But it is too like indolence to explain the *whole* of human conflict by the fall. If Adam's state was above all conflict, this was not so much due to the integrity of his nature as to the supernatural gifts in which his nature was clothed. *Per peccatum homo fit tantum homo.*[1] The conflict between sense and spirit does not arise solely for moral reasons (the original fall); its roots are ontological, in the human constitution. We have no idea what man would be like in a state of pure nature, equally unaffected by the evils of sin and by the benefits of grace; but we can be certain that in a being so complex and unequal—a converging-point of all the elements of the sensible world and of immaterial thought—a certain tension between sense and spirit would be inevitable. And in fact, by analogy, the idea of conflict can be recognised at every stage of material creation.[2] It would be easy

[1] This Augustinian aphorism does not deny the deep wounds inflicted on nature as a result of the withdrawal of original grace. Actually, man who is "no more than a man" is already less than a man.

[2] Aristotle and St Thomas have presented the negative side of this problem, emphasising the tendency to dissociation in every corruptible compound. But they paid too little attention to the positive and constructive element in conflict. It is one of the chief things to Nietzsche's credit that he contrived to some extent to rehabilitate war. Unfortunately the metaphysic of the "Will to Power" stops short at conflict as though it were a final reality. The logical result is that he makes a divinity of chaos. The whole of this metaphysic of war could be taken up again from the Christian standpoint. War is not, as Heraclitus and Nietzsche proclaimed, the "mother of all". The true root of the world is love. But terrestrial harmony thrives on

to multiply examples: positive and negative electricity in physics, the tension between the autonomic and sympathetic nerves, and that at the very heart of the endocrine system in biology. But conflict is not a final and independent reality; it is merely a subordinate "moment" of existence. Normally in every substantial whole the antagonisms and oppositions are dominated by a central peace and harmony. When limited and integrated, the conflict is healthy and profitable. But when the substantial unity of the being disintegrates, when the internal tension is no longer moderated and harnessed by some higher finality, the individual becomes the victim of anarchy and perishes. We can therefore distinguish between two kinds of conflict: the one positive and organic, the other negative and "corrupting"; the first has a tendency to preserve the vital synthesis, the second to destroy it.

What do we learn now from Christian dogma? That human nature has been *wounded* by original sin. Wounded: that means given over, not only physically, but in the very depths of its spiritual and moral being, to the attractive force of death, to succumb to all that is baneful in conflict, to everything that is negative and dissolvent. This war between the spirit and the life of the senses, which in normal conditions should

war that is latent and subjugated. All its peace contains an element of the *armed peace*. Much could be said, in connection with this general law of corruptible nature, concerning some aspects of modern pacifism, tragically unrealistic both in the political order (the sheeplike cult of peace) and in the moral (the ideal of an inner peace and harmony secured without asceticism).

make for the purifying of the senses and the temper-
ing of the will, ends in man's degradation and the
prostituting of the spirit to all his lower appetites.
The conclusion is that original sin has perverted and
"denatured", turned to corruption and disorder,
that tension between sense and spirit which we have
seen to be essentially inherent in human nature.

THE DOUBLE ASPECT OF THE LIFE OF THE SENSES

A total conflict between the senses and the spirit
is unthinkable: between two forces essentially complementary the tension can never be more than
relative. The "naked will" is a psychological myth.
Even in its fiercest battle with the senses, the spirit
is bound to rely on them for support! Its war is not
on the senses generally: it has rather the character
of an internal schism. The spirit fights *with* certain
sensuous elements that appear to be adapted and
allied to its ideal, *against* certain others that are
indifferent or opposed to it. For in the sensuous
affections there are emotions and tendencies that
foster spiritual love, there are others that rather
inhibit or blight it. It is one of the great merits of
Klages to have drawn attention to this double aspect
of human sensibility. The contemplation of a beautiful landscape, the thrill of emotion at listening to a
work of music, the image of the beloved, recalled
without shadow of physical desire, seen through a
kind of nimbus as something pure and unattainable

—such experiences are certainly sensuous,[1] but it is none the less true that sensibility such as this, so far from impeding the flight of the spirit,[2] is its inevitable complement, its nutriment and sap. On the other hand, take certain other sensuous emotions: the physical pleasure of eating, a temptation to wholly brutal sexuality, gusts of animal rage, and so on; these seem somehow foreign to our nature, hostile to our spiritual ideals and even to what we have been mentioning above, our deeper and finer emotions. Therefore, within our sensuous being, it is important to distinguish a "pole" that is ethereal, "spiritual" and pure, and another that is in the worst sense carnal and earthly. The first transcends the sensual; the second, through selfishness and lust and the vampire-like tyranny of the impulses it arouses, often plunges us even lower than the level of the animals.

We are aware that, in practice, these two aspects of the sensuous life may merge one into the other by infinitely fine degrees—sometimes conjugal love succeeds in effecting this fusion in an astonishing degree; all we maintain is that there exists between them, in the order of living experience, a heterogeneity, even a certain tension, a kind of see-saw action. The higher forms of sensibility (moral,

[1] We are not underestimating the part played here by the mind. But qualitatively what proves the importance and the *determining* rôle of the sensuous component is the fact that the mind cannot excite such emotions *ad nutum*, as it does (for example) when it is a question of resolving an arithmetical problem or using the will to make a decision.

[2] We do not deny that this higher sensibility may in turn conflict with spiritual aspirations, especially in the supernatural order. But in its essence it is none the less "allied" to spiritual love. Everything human in us has to be purified before it can be united to God.

aesthetic or religious), the spontaneous and "pre-rational" thrill that is imparted by (say) an example of heroic virtue, by a work of art or a supernatural truth—these quickly fade, as a rule, in those who give way to the pleasures of the flesh. Many a girl, for instance, has felt the change brought about in the purer, more delicate colouring of her earlier affections by contact with the "realist" satisfactions of marriage. There is something staling and cheapening in the ripe satiety of the flesh. Those dedicated to the interior life—we are intentionally passing to an extreme case—know instinctively how to discriminate between sensuous states, between those that nourish the mystical life and those that tend to disturb it. Apart from the reactions and prejudices imposed *a priori* by tradition and education, it is hardly an accident that the typical religious has a kind of aversion, an instinctive estrangement, from everything that has to do with the sexual life. There is something more in this than a good man's revulsion from sin: there is no doubt that sins, far more serious theologically, are "lived" with fewer interior qualms. It is principally this: the mystic feels that the emotions, the "temptations", of the flesh are directly menacing to a certain cenaesthetic sense[1] (a kind of "veiled trembling", a reaching down into the depths), which, though wholly distinct from religious experience in its spiritual essence, is a kind of material substratum of religious experience. It is easy to

[1] We use the word cenaesthesia, not in its current sense of organic sensibility, but much more widely: in the sense of interior sensibility, *affective consciousness*.

ridicule the Christian "phobia" of the pleasures of instinct; what is forgotten is how much this negative attitude has been the essential condition of sensuous receptivity in regard to the world of supernatural realities. Considered in isolation, judged in itself apart from its function, nothing is so rigorist and cramping as a dyke. It certainly *confines* the river— but it keeps its waters limpid and deep!

HISTORICAL REVIEW

Our instinctive life, then, appears to have two different faces: one of them, with strong sensitive feelers, seems to be "groping for" the spirit; the other —with emotions more intense, but baser and more animal—shrinks away from the spirit and exercises a disturbing effect upon it. The first makes for human synthesis, the second resists it. By experience we learn to recognise all too clearly that resistance, the recalcitrance of the carnal component of our sensuous life, to what should be the ultimate goal of the spirit.

Why this schism? Is it essential to human nature? Has it always existed? This is a serious problem in historical psychology, and all we can do here is to give a slight and incomplete outline of the solution.

If we go back in history to the earliest contacts between God and man, at the time of the Patriarchs for instance, we see that the most generous satisfaction of the instincts—the fullness of the sexual life in particular—was in harmony with the truest religious experience. Great servants of God, like Abraham and later David, had no thought of restraining their carnal instincts for the sake of safeguarding or developing their spiritual life. If these holy men ever mortified their senses, it was for a purely exterior and accidental motive: to expiate a fault or obtain some grace. Mortification was never, what it is today, a method or rule of life, a means of ensuring the inner equilibrium of the personality. To what, then, are we to attribute this harmony in ancient times between feelings that are so divergent, so often opposed, today?

The human psychosis, while it was still primitive,[1] retained certain vague traces of its original *hybris*. The elements that composed it—and this is verifiable in the earliest stages of all evolution—remained to some extent undifferentiated and mingled, shading one into another. The soul, when its pure spiritual contours were not yet clearly defined, was deeply susceptible to the biological urge: it was more carnal; the flesh, on the other hand, was far more deeply impregnated by the soul. The focus of the human synthesis was at a lower level than it is today. Man, perhaps, was more of a unity; but a unity of a lower

[1] We are aware that a lapse of time, far more considerable than that suggested by the genealogies of Genesis, intervened between the origins of humanity and the era of the Hebrew Patriarchs, and that *chronologically* Abraham was a long way off from primitive man. But given a very slow evolution of the human mentality in those self-contained societies of shepherds and husbandmen, there is good reason to think that *psychologically* a man of Abraham's time was much closer in type to primitive man than to the man of the present day.

type: a unity that was potential and germinal. He
knew nothing of the exaltation of the life of the spirit,
nothing even of what we described as "spiritualised"
sensuous pleasure. As against this, his instinctive
and carnal life developed in its own way with a kind
of tranquil and poetic completeness, today hardly
conceivable. In the primitive soul the religious ideal,
the appeal of the divine, was akin to the primitive
rhythms of nature; it was a continuation of them.
God was "lived" as the summit of cosmic experience,
as the transfiguring of it. "The human consciousness
was still in twilight and confused," says Raïssa
Maritain with considerable acumen; "it was still
close to the great elemental instincts like the con-
servation and propagation of life. . . . Grace was
present and active, but in the manner of a vital
impulse: *it was as though it disguised itself as nature.*"[1]
Conflict at this infant stage of humanity was still
slumbering.

Even in the most rigidly "naturalist" history there
can be no denying the central influence that has been
exerted by Christianity. One fact is obvious; the
monumental peace and inner unity of ancient man[2]
was shattered by the ideal brought into the world by
Christ. Between the demands of the soul and the
demands of the senses, of life and nature, this ideal
of Christ's opened up an abyss of tears, an abyss to

[1] In her study of sanctity in the state of nature, *Nova et vetera*, 1935,
No. 3, p. 243.
[2] This does not exclude a certain latent disequilibrium, due to the
fact of original sin. But pre-Christian man had not the felt experience of it that St Paul was to have (Rom. 7).

be filled with the sacrifices of millions. Such a work of dislocation may at first seem shocking; but there is just as much cause to blame the force of germination for "separating" the roots and stem of a plant, from dragging in different directions what were originally united in the undifferentiated substance of the seed. God is spirit: he exacts worship, no longer "on this mountain nor yet at Jerusalem"—symbols of the adherence of religion to the senses and nature—but "in spirit and in truth". Christ's appeal gave a new centre to the human consciousness; it gave it freedom to feel the specific and sovereign attraction of the spirit—of the spirit in its late development, jealous and supreme, soaring high above those primitive and circumscribed manifestations of it, the technical intelligence of the scientist, the philosopher's logic or the conqueror's will to power. This is none other than spiritual love. Conceive the tension created in man by the magnetism of this new centre! Primitive sensibility, fed on flesh and blood, so close to the bowels of material creation, could not adapt itself, as it was, to a love disincarnate. Before any new synthesis of the human being could be realised, the distance between the old centre and the new had to be acknowledged; and so too had the tension. This migration, from the centre of human impulses towards the purity of the spirit, towards God, is the thing that is the essence of Christian asceticism. It has doubly transformed the quality of sensuous life: on the one hand it has clarified, refined and disciplined the instincts; on the other, wherever rebel instinct, rooted in its material polarity, has stubbornly resisted this integrating process, it has repressed and punished it, thrust it ever farther from the centre and "soul" of the individual. This is the explanation of the phenomenon we have already stressed, that double polarity of the sensuous appetite. But these two influences of the spirit on the senses— the one attractive, the other repulsive—however contrary they may appear at first sight, are really correlative and co-operative, and that in a very precise way. This ascetical rupture or dichotomy leads to a future synthesis; it is the first stage of it. Every healthy war is a kind of connecting-link between a lower and a higher peace. In so far as the instincts are checked in their totalitarian demands and so deprived of their centralised power, the fundamental need for unity—the need that governs every animate creature—is a standing invitation to enter the orbit of the spirit and to submit to its governance. In every synthesis achieved, the lower elements, in order to unite harmoniously with the "dominant", with the soul of the synthesis, must first be (as it were) dispossessed of their own being: they must first be "conquered", reduced to mere virtuality.[1]

THREE PHASES

There are three phases in this evolution and we may distinguish them thus:

[1] For man, this inner evolution confirms, in the order of the concrete and the "lived", the ontological definition of his soul: *formally* spiritual, *virtually* sensuous.

1. The primitive state, in which the lower and the higher merge one into the other, with a certain predominance of the concrete and lower;

2. The severance of the higher from the lower, with its resulting conflicts;

3. The unity of the differentiated being, where the higher and the lower share a final harmony governed by the higher.[1]

We are perfectly aware that this scheme is "ideal". The harmony, sought by asceticism, is realised in this world only in varying degrees, according to epochs and individuals, and according to general trends in morals or ideas; it is never perfect, unfortunately. We have no hopes that humanity will ever attain a golden age, in which conflicts will come to an end and result in complete harmony: asceticism will always be necessary to the children of Adam. But the facts themselves are unaffected by such pessimism. Even if asceticism is never to be transcended on earth (transcended upwards, I mean: it is easily transcended downwards) its ancillary and provisional character remains the same.

Not that we would underestimate the price that mankind has had to pay for the vast reversal of values Christianity has brought about. Between the normal end of a vital process and the result actually

[1] What is involved here is a universal law of the sensible world, which *by analogy* can be applied even to the supernatural order (in so far as this order is incarnated in man). Hans André, in his admirable studies in experimental biology, has revealed the existence of this tendency to transcend conflict, the "dead point" inherent in organic nature.

obtained, matter and sin may erect all kinds of ugly barriers. The dangerous stages of transition—conflict, division, suffering—that should normally hasten and consolidate the inner unity of the soul, have only to "miscarry" or degenerate very slightly, or be exalted by the individual to the status of idols, to have tragic results in dangerously false psychological situations. But how could this prodigy be accomplished—the raising of man, a being compounded of the inertia of flesh and the poison of sin, to the pure life of God— without the incurring of terrible defeats and disasters? A horror of life and instinct, narrow and hideous asceticism, a sclerosis of sense and spirit in mutual isolation—all these, it is true, may have been some of the results; but they were not so much due to Christianity itself as to the ungrateful soil in which the seed was sown. And all this, too, has its positive side. If many ascetics warred ferociously against their instincts, the reason was that they felt them to be still too crude to be integrated or even "recognised" by the spirit, a perilous threat to the appeal of the divine and to the very life of their souls. Better an unseemly brawl than the total surrendering of one's soul to the beast—even if it were only to the beast within! A similar defence could be made for the universal contempt in which many religious hold the realities of life. Their errors, foolish enough though they are from the ontological standpoint, have yet a certain *polemical* value. Those who make war use calumnies against the enemy to foster the "offensive spirit"! Iron has many uses other than to be forged into fetters, but we can hardly expect a convict to appreciate it.[1]

"Christianity", wrote Nietzsche, "gave Eros a dose of poison: he did not die of it, but degenerated into Vice." As a criticism of the influence of Christianity on the sexual life, this wilfully ignores the highly important credit side of the transaction. If, in medieval and modern times, sexual life has become spiritualised, if it has reached a degree of depth and constancy unknown in antiquity, there is only one thing that accounts for it: the purifying effect of Christian asceticism. It would be easy to enlarge on the fact that "chivalrous love", the feelings of respect and loyalty to woman, have also their only origin in Christianity. In our days, the development of the religious life—even the mystical life—among those who are married, the actual absorbing of the joys of the flesh into divine charity itself, seems a very happy

[1] It has long been remarked that man has an invincible tendency to deify all he loves. Less attention has been given to the opposite process, which consists in "demonising", making an absolute evil of what he detests and combats.

We are perfectly aware of the residue of folly that the Christian idea of purity has left in certain ages and individuals. The higher the ideal the more ludicrous its distortion. We are somewhat embarrassed, for instance, when we find a great Catholic moralist using the adjective *turpis* to describe the joys of marriage. This absurd "deposit" of asceticism was most muddy and dense in the nineteenth century—the influence of decadent Jansenism is very evident here. There would be no point in multiplying instances of this state of mind but we may quote one rather amusing case. Towards the end of the last century, a little girl (now an old woman) was sent as a boarder to a school conducted by nuns. During class, on one of her first days there, she ventured to confide in her mistress: "Sister, I have a pain in my tummy." "Child," replied the Sister, "that's an indecent expression. You should have said: 'I have a pain under my apron.' "

augury of the final transcending of these negative dregs of asceticism, as well as of the human synthesis and "interior Catholicism" to which we may confidently look forward in the future. Nietzsche's aphorism touches only the reverse side of the problem, the human side. The moment Christianity had presented man with a new ideal, a new centre, the instincts that could not adapt themselves to this spiritual revolution obviously could be satisfied no longer with that innocence and "good conscience", with that acquiescence of the whole being, that had been adequate for antiquity. That was how sensuality tended to become undisciplined and rebellious, experienced more and more as something disturbing and impure—in fact, as "vice". Nothing primitive, indeed, is so base and abject, so utterly vulgar, as a modern man surrendering to the primacy of the senses. This is a rule without exception. A lost synthesis is something worse than primordial *hybris*. Wherever Christianity begins and fails—and this applies to peoples and individuals alike—man descends far lower than his condition in antiquity. "The last state of that man is worse than the first."

Christianity is not the enemy of life. The Church has condemned the Jansenist sacrilege of anathematising creation. Christianity is not "inhuman", unless the human centre of gravity is situated too low; it is not opposed to life, except to the precise extent that the life of the senses conflicts with the love of the spirit and preys upon it.

THE NOTION OF SUBLIMATION

Perhaps some excuse should be pleaded for using this Freudian expression. Actually we can find none better. In any case, we are not employing it in the Freudian sense. Words have very little importance in themselves; the thing that matters is their intellectual content.

Sublimation, as we see it, is the most perfect relationship between the senses and the spirit, the realisation (or at least a partial one) of that inner synthesis slowly achieved, as we have seen, by means of the pangs of asceticism.

To start with facts. Let us take two forms of spiritual love, different in kind it is true, but both of them genuinely supersensible: the inspiration of a poet singing of God and the utterances of a mystic in communion with God. Each employs terms derived from the flesh or the senses—sometimes even from sexual life. Their entire being thrills; their whole nature seems to share in their transcendent emotion. Now, in the genesis of these higher states, what is the part played by the instincts and impulses of the flesh?

Here we are confronted with two interpretations. According to the Freudian, these states described as "higher" are simply transferences of the instinct: devious expedients of sensuality, inhibited from its normal exercise, to find some veiled and insidious satisfaction. The artistic or religious ideal is a mere masking of the instinct. All human rapture is sensual in its nature.

To this the anti-Freudian will reply (we have found many such arguments in Catholic writers): The term sublimation conceals an ambiguity. Sensibility is incapable of being transformed into spirit. Poetic or religious rapture is purely spiritual in its nature. When a man turns away from sensual pleasures to concentrate all his passion on an ideal, he does not "sublimate" his instincts into ideals, he merely changes his interests and aims, he passes from a lower level of activity to one that is higher. Between these two states there is no continuity. If the ideal uses expressions derived from the instincts and human life, that is due entirely to the nature of human language, which must shape its notions with the aid of sensible data. Sensible comparisons have here only a symbolic value: in the ideal and its rapture, the senses, as such, play no part at all.

The second explanation is sounder than the first; but it goes too far. Freudianism degrades man and calumniates the spirit; but its adversaries underestimate the unity of human action and at the same time they malign the instinct. In man there is always spirit as well as animality; but it is also true that there is no animality wholly separated from spirit. To absorb the higher into the lower is certainly foolish, but to part the two is inhuman. There are three possible views of the psychological processes included by Freud under the term "sublimation". By means of instinct, says Freud. In spite of instinct, is the rejoinder of certain "spiritualists". But what we say is: *with* instinct. Man is a human being; we know of no ideals that can be said to be *purely* the masks of instinct. Nothing is more ridiculous than the complacent over-simplification with which your Freudian, confronted with a higher psychological state, murmurs: "You can't deceive me: you are just a pretty mask!" On the other hand we have no experience of human harmony or fulfilment that has not its specific contribution of instinct.

What we mean is this. If there is nothing in human instincts to distinguish them from animal instincts—as the arguments of our hyperspiritualists would lead us to suppose—no intimate collaboration between sense and spirit is possible, therefore no sublimation. But this is not the case. Our instincts are akin to spirit; they are made for it. Their true centre, the inwardness of their nature, is on a higher level than the finalities of organic life. "The carnal appetite", as a psychologist has pointed out, "is the essence of our sexual life, but it does not measure its depths. High above the narrow track of animal desire there soars a radiant tenderness that has nothing in common with the world of space. The soul also is endowed with sex. . . ."[1] When we speak of the

[1] Freud has rightly insisted on the difference between the *genital* and the *sexual*. Human sexuality goes far beyond the instinct for procreation. There is a supra-genital sexuality. Its rôle has a vast importance in the engendering of the higher affective states, artistic creation and even mystical love. On this latter point it is as well to guard against over-simplification. But it is impossible to deny the fact that the beginnings of mystical love very frequently coincide with the first awakenings of the sexual life—pure as these are, and experienced rather more in the soul than in the flesh. The crisis of puberty, especially in girls, is very congenial to religious experiences. In the same way, the dawning of a conversion has often a certain

instinct's part in the process of sublimation we do not mean the instinct in its animal polarity, but the instinct suffused with this delicate radiance, in vibrant communion with the spirit.

Sublimation may be conceived as a kind of upward return of the instinct towards the human being's immaterial origins, a sort of *qualitative* integration of sensuous rhythms into the pure melody of the interior life. Subjectively it is accompanied by a feeling of balance, of an inner peace and fulfilment, of deliverance from servitude and discord where the lower appetites are concerned, as though the depths of one's nature had grown suddenly transparent to the rays of the ideal.

In a revolution such as this there is more than a change of practical interests, more than a new orientation. All change, all conversion is not formally

colouring of sex. Naturally, though it already transcends what may be properly called instinct, this remains as yet very imperfectly sublimated, and the evolution of divine love subjects it to the night of the senses. (Cf. the passages in St John of the Cross about the "spiritual sensuality" of neophytes.) Every human being is impregnated with sex, and the affective tone of feminine love, even when still more spiritual, will always be different from that of the male. (Of course we are not discussing here anything outside the limits of strict material causality.) It must also be observed that when this supra-genital sexuality passes, what follows is not a mere descent to the genital instinct of the animal but to something far lower. Parted from its human *depths*, from its spiritual harmony, sex is also severed from its animal *essence*. Flesh without soul, it degenerates into debauchery, into a flat brutal lust that dries up the milk of the interior life, and into various aberrations utterly false to the procreative ends of the animal instinct. This is infra-genital sexuality, something debarred from the purely genital equilibrium of the animal. When it is not transcended upwards, it is transcended downwards. To adapt Pascal's saying: "Who ceases to be an angel becomes less than a beast."

accompanied by sublimation. A man who yesterday was in the thrall of the flesh, even entirely dominated by it, may conquer it today and impose on himself a wholly spiritual way of life. To resist the assaults of temptation he may mortify himself, take up some study or perform physical exercises. Certainly a considerable part of the nervous energy and physiological reserves that were consumed before in satisfying sexual needs will now be healthily employed. But all this concerns merely the most "neutral" of forces, the most animal, the least "qualified" of all in the organic life. Specifically and qualitatively, there will be no concurrence of the instinct in such ascetical manœuvres; rather the instinct will be bullied by the ideal, as it were paralysed and deadened by it; fundamentally it will remain just as much estranged from it as ever. Such is the case with the conventional ascetic who conquers the rebel flesh only to be tormented by it in turn. Admittedly the change is profound, but the sublimation is nil. On the other hand, if one day the same man feels an appeasement of his inward tension, if images and memories, so recently mutinous and "culpable", are suddenly stripped of their skin of turbid emotions and appear transfigured, as feelings that are the *aura* and prolongation of spiritual love, then we shall have an instance of genuine sublimation. In the first case the instinct is merely dominated; in the second it is integrated by the spirit.

It is the latter phenomenon that Freud calls sublimation. We need not delay over his cheap and "economic" interpretation of the process. Instinct does not create spirit, but it is permeable by the spirit. An unsatisfied instinct could never "change" into an ideal,[1] but the ideal can attract the instinct into its orbit. Sublimation leads to the development of aptitudes contained in instinct, to the spiritualisation and hypertrophy of the "mind-tendency" in the flesh. Instinct is no longer merely daunted, it is made tractable; it serves the ideal with the finer element of its nature, the soul of it uplifted by a higher attraction. Sublimated instinct is like a cloud traversed by the rays of the sun: the water composing it has lost nothing of its own nature; the heavenly body has simply raised it above all gross contact with earth and completely suffused it with light. Or it is like a flower, almost perished but still fragrant: it retains everything of itself that is purest and most precious, only its harsh material definition has been lost. If it were not for the unfortunate use that has been made of it, the Freudian term *übertragen* (transposition or transference) would be the most illuminating to use. "To carry beyond"—no formula could better express the profound action of the soul whereby this instinct is attuned and "focalised" outside itself.[2] In an existence consecrated to the

[1] The very term "sublimation of instinct" implies the existence and attractive force of faculties that transcend instinct. An unsatisfied instinct can become atrophied by lack of use or exasperated by privation. But if there is nothing higher than itself, how could it result, by the sole fact of being crossed, in the state of fulfilment and harmony that characterises sublimation?

[2] We are speaking here in terms of character-experience, not rational psychology. Far be it from us to contest the radical heterogeneity of instinctive and spiritual acts! We could couple our

explanation with the passages in St Thomas about the *redundantia* of the spirit upon the senses. We simply repeat that the instinct we are speaking of is not instinct in its purely animal form (in the synthetic order of action, this could never appear alone) but instinct exalted by infiltrations of the spirit. It is a commonplace of Thomism that, in the functional order, a higher cause can influence a lower cause (and thereby transfigure and "sublimate" it) without altering the actual nature of the lower cause. Besides, to speak of a *specific* concurrence of instinct in the genesis of certain states of spiritual fulfilment is not to diminish the *accessory* character of this concurrence. The conductive element is always that of the spirit: sublimation occurs when the sensibility is in tune with it. If we take the extreme case—which only a Catholic psychologist can do—we have the resurrection and glorifying of the body. That is the full and perfect example of what we mean by sublimation. The elect will preserve a life that is specifically and *actually* instinctive. But their instincts will be disengaged, to a perfect degree, from the material finalities of the world; in other words, they will be perfectly spiritualised. When Christ replied to the dull-witted objections of the Jews that the blessed "will be like the angels of God", this does not mean that they will be desexualised like the angels, but that their sexuality will be stripped of the animal polarity, the genital character it has in this world. Such a harmony can and ought to be encouraged even here. This is how St John of the Cross defines (incidentally) the meaning and extent of the sublimating process, considered here in connection with the mystical synthesis of man: "And there follows: 'And the cavalry came down at the sight of the waters.' By the waters are here understood the spiritual delights and blessings whereof in this estate the soul has fruition inwardly with God. By the cavalry are here understood the faculties of the sensual part, both interior and exterior. These, says the Bride here, come down in this estate at the sight of the spiritual waters, for the lower and sensual part of the soul is now *so purified and in some manner spiritualised* that she, together with her sensual faculties and natural forces, is recollected and has participation and fruition, after her manner, of the spiritual grandeurs which God is communicating to the soul, even as David signified when he said: *cor meum et caro mea exsultaverunt in Deum vivum.* And it is to be noted that the Bride says not here that the cavalry came down to taste of the waters but that it came down at the sight of them; for the sensual part with its faculties has not the capacity to taste essentially and properly of spiritual blessings . . . but through a certain overflowing of the spirit they receive in the senses refreshment and delight therefrom . . ." It should be noticed that even the pleasures of the flesh may be experienced, when they profoundly accord with the spirit, without any lowering of the interior life. If it were not for the matter of sin, this unity should be the rule in Christian marriage.

ideal, the coefficient of permeability, of the "tracta-
bility" of the instinct, determines very largely the
coefficient of harmony and joy in the interior life.
Here rather more precision is called for. The capacity for spiritualising the instinct depends essentially
on the quality of the instinct, not on that of the will.
A strong will can directly dominate, but it cannot
integrate the instinct. There is no correlation
between strength of will and the *possibilities* of
sublimation. Those with heroic will-power may keep
their instinct enchained all their lives, but without
any relief from interior conflict, without any appreciable sublimation: this is the case with natural
ascetics—some Stoics, for instance. On the other
hand, there can be a fine interpenetration of instinct
and spirit in subjects whose will-power is anything
but outstanding—particularly in temperaments
naturally inclined to mystical passivity. Moreover
the process of sublimation takes place outside the
will's immediate influence and control. All the will
can do here is to *prepare*, by patiently resisting the
carnal exteriorisations of instinct, for the awakening
of natural aptitudes, for the sublimation *already
existing* in the instinct. If these aptitudes do not
exist (actually they exist always, but sometimes in a
practically negligible degree) the individual will
never arrive at a relative harmony except by the
wearing down of the instinct. This explains the
emotional sterility and dryness of certain predomi-
nantly "spiritual" types: hyperintellectualists, for
instance, or those whose philosophy centres wholly in

the will. Here the price of interior peace and unity is the drying up of the springs of instinct. Only by sublimation is it possible to escape the degrading consequences of domination by the instinct, the vulgarity and constraints of the flesh, and at the same time lose nothing of the resources and spontaneity that belong to the life of the senses.[1]

MIXED SENTIMENTS AND INTERIOR ILLUSION

What we have just been describing is the most desirable, ultimately the ideal, state of affairs. Conditions, in practice, are rarely so favourable. Every interpenetration of sense and spirit is not necessarily a sublimation; there are states of inner satisfaction that are morally and ontologically far below the level of conflict. Two examples will serve to illustrate this point. Consider, on the one hand, a saint like Teresa in a moment of mystical fulfilment; on the other, Dr Janet's *Madeleine* in one of her states of "ravishment". The entire sensibility of both seems vibrant; both express their rapture in terms one associates with the senses and even with the flesh. Yet any psychologist who is competent to pass a *synthetic* judgement will get the impression, in the first case, of purity and unity, whereas in the second he will have a feeling of uneasiness and suspicion. The sensibility of St Teresa seems to be invaded by

[1] As against Freudian pansexualism, we maintain that the sublimating process may be applied to instincts other than the sexual. But it remains a fact that the sexual and maternal instincts are those which *qualitatively* lend themselves best to sublimation.

God; that of Madeleine appears to be seeking a satisfaction, perverse and unhealthy in itself, but usurping the name of God. St Teresa's psychological state reveals a sublimation of the highest order; the feelings of our pseudo-mystic may best be described by what Dostoevsky (that amazing psychologist) calls a "mixed sentiment".

In such a psychological state we may discover the tangled influences of two separate causes: one seems to be ontological, the other rather of the moral order.[1]

Today mixed sentiments are one of the plagues of the interior life. More than the grossest selfishness, more than any brutal and flagrant concupiscence of the flesh, they impair and paralyse man's ascent to the ideal. To return to what we said before about the inner synthesis of the human being: every severance, every conflict, has for its end the attainment of some higher unity. But where this process miscarries—through some failure in the vital potential of the individual, of the family or of the race—man falls far below the level of his starting-point. His lost spiritual harmony is replaced by a new

[1] The terms are not used here in their strict philosophical sense. By "ontological" we mean inevitable, constitutional, independent of choice and liberty; by moral, what is subject (at least relatively) to the influence of the will. Similarly the terms synthesis and *hybris* are not applied in this study to the human being as a metaphysical unity, a substance; they serve simply to designate certain ways in which this substance is manifested while it is still immersed in the dynamic "becoming". The Hegelian triad (being, first indeterminate, then in conflict with itself in order to reunite later in a higher synthesis) does not govern the changeless world of essences as such but it is profoundly significant in connection with their concrete, historical and phenomenal realisation.

hybris. This is no longer the primitive *hybris*, nurtured healthily on elemental resources, but the sterile *hybris* of the decrepit. The sentiments of modern mystagogues, however archaic the colouring of their outer surface, have no more resemblance to those of the primitive than have an old man's maunderings to the babbling of an infant. In this state of inner disintegration, sentiments tend to lose their specific exactness and definition; perverted, vague, crumbling, incapable both of uniting hierarchically and of opposing one another in healthy conflict, they become reduced to a condition of hopeless confusion. Flesh and spirit confound their respective finalities in an indeterminate *tertium quid*; the former never fulfils its animal impulses; the latter turns false to its own immaterial ends, with the inevitable result that it is swallowed up in the flesh. Such is the upshot of this perverted procedure: a union without unity. To understand the rôle of the sensibility in spiritual love it is necessary to know how to distinguish between sublimation and mixed sentiment: the first is a synthesis: a refining, uplifting and *informing* by the ideal; the other is a hotch-potch: a muddling and confusing of the ideal with the sensibility.

We may illustrate this with a very clear example. Here is a glass of good wine. It contains water, and in a high proportion. But no one would dream of saying: This liquid is a mixture of water, alcohol, tannin and so on. It would simply be called wine. The form or "soul" of wine dominates, uplifts and integrates the nature of the water. On the other hand, take diluted wine: outwardly the mixture has a close resemblance to wine, but it is really water *usurping* the name of wine; not only so, but it changes, thins down and degrades the actual wine it is in contact with. Similarly an ideal transfiguring the sensibility is a very different thing from a "diluted" ideal, sophisticated by degenerate sensibility. There we have St Teresa: here our hospital-ward mystic. . . .

In terms of conscience and morals, perhaps, one might translate "mixed sentiment" by "interior illusion". There is, in fact, an affective tendency that, when allied to a basic weakness of character, is a veritable hotbed of mixed sentiments: it is the *instinctive refusal of truth.*

This inward untruth usually depends to a large extent on causes outside the individual's control. It frequently has its roots in abnormal repressions; these may be due to heredity, tradition, education, or just a general psychological atmosphere. Man, in the past, has been too inclined to play the angel. Primary tendencies of the living being (the sexual instinct above all—we have explained the "polemical" motive behind this) have been considered fundamentally vile and impure, both anti-spiritual and anti-divine. Men have grown accustomed, little by little, not only to dominate these tendencies but to disown them altogether, to banish them beyond the frontiers of consciousness as though they were highly undesirable aliens. The result might have been guessed: the volitional synthesis has only to flag, carnal incitements have only to infiltrate into the zone of consciousness, into the zone of immediate action—a common enough occurrence with feeble characters—and the instinct that has been ignored or "demonised" *a priori* will be sure to reappear wearing the mask of an angel!

In addition to this influence, which is social in origin, there is the reaction of the ego against all that is lacking or unstable in its vitality. The more a man becomes aware of the poverty and impurity of his inner life, the greater his compensating need to trick it out in ideal colours. This phenomenon is the principal characteristic of the neurotic; it is found, almost invariably, at the root of the pseudo-mysticisms and religious illusions of our time. Neurosis— the heavy price we pay for civilisation and culture— is the malady of the flesh in its most intimate and immediate contact with the spirit. Unlike purely physiological complaints, it creeps up into the very threshold of the immaterial, the subtle fringes of the sensibility that overlap thought, the mysterious confluence of soul and body. It leaves man life, but it robs him of all subjective fulfilment, it prevents his *living* the purity and resources of his life; and naturally, by so doing, it provokes the deepest and most incurable reactions of the wounded ego.

This type of exhausted and compensative neurotic is one that seems to have appeared fairly late in history. It is therefore important to distinguish between religious illusion as we see it in the remote past—in the Middle Ages, for instance—and the false mysticism that appears to be peculiar to modern times. There is no doubt that in both cases an "impure" mixture of sense and spirit is involved. But a careful study of particular *illuminati* or heresiarchs of the past gives the impression of an *excess of vitality uncontrolled by the spirit*; on the other hand, your modern pseudo-mystic seems rather to present a spectacle of *lack of vitality compensated by spiritual illusion*. This is the explanation, perhaps, of the very slender influence, the lack of "social radiation", of modern mystagogues compared with the vital magnetism and collective ascendancy possessed, it would seem, by so many of their predecessors.

Naturally, in these perverted and decadent souls, mixed sentiments are always defined, and "registered" by consciousness, under the title of some more imposing component—even if this be but a dream or a memory, or a flash of enlightenment. The moral falsehood—the mask disguising the absence of true unity and sublimity—compensates self-esteem for the ontological lie, involved by the fact of being somehow predisposed to sentiments in reality so hybrid and indeterminate.

Here we must be more exact. How are we to distinguish the sublimation of a saint from the impure *hybris* of the neuropath? An eminent philosopher, who is also an excellent psychoanalyst, was once discussing with me certain episodes, charged with sensuous symbolism, in the religious experience of St Teresa. "I would not undertake", he remarked, "to defend such symbolism in the presence of a psychoanalyst." On reflection, I agreed. *Analytically*, such states are certainly indefensible. The water an analyst extracts from a glass of Clos-Vougeot is no different from the water in adulterated wine. In the same way, when isolated, "congealed" (as it were) by psychological analysis, the sexual symbolism of the *Song of Songs*, or one of St Teresa's ecstasies, may be identified with that of any neurotic female who happens to be the victim of religious hallucinations. But what we are concerned with here is not the separate existence of such a symbolism or experience, it is its position and function in the whole individual in whom it is integrated. Psychological analysis, by making an arbitrary cut, by actualising elements that are mingled, virtualised in a synthetic complex and having their supreme reality in their relationship with the organic whole—something that is entirely outside themselves—is basically guilty of a lack of realism. Only by employing *synthetic* criteria is it possible to judge fundamentally in this matter. It is only by the total resonance (full or empty, pure or impure, harmonious or discordant) of the whole personality that we can interpret the isolated sensuous note; not vice versa. We are aware of the difficulties and limitations of the synthetic method. The understanding of a living whole (always obscure and imperfect) calls for something more than mere intellectual penetration: it requires emotional sympathy. Consequently it is always in danger of subjectivism and lends itself very ill to universal demonstration. From the point of view of abstract confirmation, the analytical method has all the advantages; it has logic in its favour, at any rate the charm of a superficial (and somewhat showy) logic, and solutions within the capacity of the most mediocre brains. But if it is true that substance and totality are categories inevitably inherent in all nature, and *a fortiori* in animate nature, these brilliant analytical conclusions are obtained by "denaturing" the psychological fact. In the case we are dealing with, the analyst sees clearly in spiritual love the *presence* of a sensible component; he sees the proximity, the osmosis, between the senses and the ideal; what he does not know—and this alone is important—is whether it is the senses that have risen to the level of the ideal, or whether the ideal has flagged, and so served as a "pretext" and mask for the senses.

Introspectively, the true sublimation of the sensibility is recognised by two signs: the sensuous pleasure, so far from being "monopolist" or self-enclosed, out of tune with the ideal, actually fortifies and enriches the spiritual love (this consonance, according to John of the Cross, is the criterion of the purity of love for creatures . . .); not only so, but the soul experiences a sovereign independence in regard to the effusions of the spiritualised senses. The criterion is absolute: the higher and purer the joys of the senses, the more freely the spirit accepts or sacrifices them. In the sublimated passion there is an essential orientation towards sacrifice. No paradox, this: the senses no longer reject sacrifice, because their treasure, the soul and centre of their rapture, lies outside themselves! On the other hand, in perverse affections the soul appears to be numbed both to the joys and to the sorrows of the sensibility.

As in the case of sublimation before, what we have been describing is an extreme case: namely, mixed sentiment as it is encountered in morbid and decadent subjects. In practice—and especially at the period of puberty or incipient conversion—there are mixed sentiments that are by no means neurotic in character. Psychologically they can be placed somewhere between primitive indeterminism and a larval sublimation. What we have to do with here is not decadent sensuality morbidly usurping the ideal, but an ideal too much the prisoner of sensible emotions, still imperfectly disengaged from its carnal swaddling-clothes.[1] Such a state results normally

[1] An extreme opposition between sense and spirit is much less in evidence among women than among men; the point where the sensibility becomes sublimated is consequently lower in the feminine character. One has only to compare the degree of release from sensible pleasure in St Teresa at a particular period of her mystical life with that in St John of the Cross at a similar stage. To become integrated in spiritual love, the "vibrations" of feminine sensibility do not need to be so strictly "decanted" as those of the masculine passions. This may lead some men astray when they estimate a woman's character. It must not be forgotten that if a woman's mind is less disengaged from ties of flesh and blood, her instincts are more akin to the things of the soul. Men are inclined to be severe judges of feminine states in which they detect an excessive "proximity" between the sensibility and spiritual love, for no other reason than that the same "proximity" in a man could be nothing else but an impure transposition. Naturally this does not mean that women are exempt from illusions. (There is no intention, by the way, to discuss in this note any but the proximity of sense to spirit inherent in a true sublimation.) Actually the supra-carnal tone of their instincts is something that predisposes them to illusion. All we mean is that,

in the purifying of the senses, thus preparing the
ground for a new synthesis of love, securely centred
amid the loftiest peaks of the spirit. Among Orientals
(and especially among the Slavs) in whom the elemental frothing of life goes with an imperfect
evolution of the rational faculties, mixed sentiments
are much more general than in Western man.[1]
Besides, however impure a mixed sentiment may be,
in practice there is no such thing as an absolute
illusion or an absolute mask. Where is the coiner
who has never handled a genuine gold piece? The
pure Pharisee is below all conflict and illusion. There
is always discoverable, in neurotics who pretend to
some particular ideal, a certain aptitude for experi-
encing the ideal in question—even though the manner
of it is tenuous and intermittent, incapable of anything like habitual realisation. The ego attaches

when submitted to criteria drawn from the male experience alone,
entirely pure osmoses between a woman's instincts and her ideal
stand in constant danger of being condemned. It should be added,
too, that woman possesses an instinct unknown to man, the maternal
instinct; manifestations of this, when more or less "transposed", are
often attributed by men to sexuality.

[1] The Western (and above all the Latin) character, strongly
polarised normally towards spiritual unity and precision, sees
mixed sentiments as a symptom of psychological degeneracy. It is
worth observing, too, that it is fundamentally sceptical of the ontological existence of mixed sentiments: it tends to attribute their
manifestations to hypocritical design. We have only to think of the
meaning—entirely moral, and also uncomplimentary—which we
give to the word *duplicity*. When the actions of an individual seem
to conflict with this passion for unity and lucidity, the Latin mind
tends naturally to suspect a conscious and deliberate lie! This
satisfies its fundamental desire for simplicity. Molière, in *Tartuffe*,
succeeds in describing the comedian in the guise of the saint; he could
never have described, as Dostoevsky did so often, the inward mingling
of saint and comedian.

itself greedily to this fragile experience, erecting, as soon as it fades, an elaborate scaffolding of illusions in an endeavour to restore it to life and amplify it further.

CONCLUSION

Our examination of the subject so far may be summarised thus: the human problem is not one of choosing between sense and spirit, but between the *domination* of the senses and the domination of the spirit. It is not a question of rigidly excluding a particular form of human life, but of knowing which of its various forms is the one that should occupy the central position and exert a guiding attraction on the rest. There is no such thing as the alternative: "for or against the senses". The glory of Catholic thought is to be against nothing at all (unless it be the evil that is merely nothingness) but to be *for* everything— provided it accepts its place and its appropriate bounds.

In conjugal, maternal or mystical love, however essentially different the human and sensible components, the evolution of each towards perfection and harmony is none the less subject to a common necessity: no affection can remain true, no affection can remain pure, unless the human component "accords" with divine love. Among the conditions of this agreement there are two which seem to lie at the very heart of our destiny: truth and suffering.

"The truth will set you free," said Christ. "All dissembled truth grows poisonous"—in terms of concrete psychology, the saying of Nietzsche is almost a continuation of the Gospel text. It seems certain—since every historical process has its supernatural finality—that the function of the "awakening" that characterises the modern age, extraordinary as it is and sometimes catastrophic, is to prepare for a new era of spiritual love, freer and purer than anything we have known before. At the root of all harmful repressions, all impure transpositions of sensuality, there may always be discerned an attitude of negation, a flight from reality. The only means man has to escape these evils is to be true to himself: the whole of his inner universe must be humbly accepted into his consciousness and his love. Quickened and exalted by supernatural love, the consciousness can "redeem" the murky depths into which it descends. Moreover the necessity for inner truth is closely bound up with the necessity for detachment: the process of "stripping", in regard to the senses, that is the lesson of St John of the Cross. The soul must either mingle its sensibility with divine love or it must suspect and repress the sensibility as a demon; in both cases it remains bound and hypnotised by the senses. Interior liberty is stifled by illusion. True, there are graceless characters that must ever be at war with their passions; but it is possible to fight without creating phantoms. This recognition of our inner truth, this "adopting" of it, is no guarantee of an ending to conflicts, but it purifies them of such elements as are warped or poisonous. In the very heart of conflict there is always a way of preserving peace and transcending conflict. We know how heroically difficult this inner loyalty may be to some: in a neurotic consciousness, for instance, which makes illusions of all its reasons for existence, the rays of truth are as piercing as death and despair. But if a means can be found of opening a way and persevering in it, a spirituality may be born, unhampered by any complicity of the flesh and able to accept an inward poverty and sterility such as the normal man could scarcely conceive. Such a spirituality may be very pure and very deep. As an extreme case of this, we may quote a fine passage from Gertrude von Le Fort: "It is better to die of the truth created by God than to live on lies created by oneself." What is the good of living on illusions, when God loves and awaits the whole truth that is in us? What pride can only mask, love and grace can sanctify. Nothing is so debased, nothing so befouled, that it cannot be redeemed by the kiss of Christ. All our misery can be *fused* in God. The tragedy of pride and illusion is to *confuse* it with God.[1]

The process of spiritualising the sensuous affections, which we have described above by the term "sublimation", can be finally accomplished only in

[1] We do not mean that *every* man may usefully know *the whole* of his misery. Truth cannot be morally and supernaturally fruitful unless it be accepted in divine simplicity and love. Separated from the first command of the decalogue, the Socratic precept "Know thyself" is bound to engender nihilism and despair. Knowledge of self is good only to the soul that is God's captive. Without God, man lives by illusion and dies from interior truth; with the saint it is the other way about.

suffering and by means of it. It was supernatural wisdom, as well as psychological intuition, that made John of the Cross put the "night of the senses" at the very threshold of the mystical life. The senses are the cradle of the ideal; but when we become attached to their delights, they quickly become its tomb. In every deep affection the sensuous element, when it has not as yet been worked upon by suffering, has something limited and imprudent about it, a kind of base euphoria, the smoke of which clouds the flame of spiritual penetration and greatly weakens its power. "Woe upon you who laugh now," Christ said. This was no condemnation of joy in itself, but of that idolatrous mundane happiness that has not yet learned to smile through tears. It is the Cross that refines and mellows the passions; it strips them, not of their individual and personal quality, but of that narrowness and ugly "particularity", which is the price that has to be paid for sensuous individualism; it gives them a kind of vesperal transparence and repose, fits them for communion with the universal, for prolonging, without break or falsification, the full enchantment of immaterial love. The word "temperance", at first sight so commonplace, stands admirably for this spiritual saturation of the senses, this peace-giving synthesis of light and flame.

Suffering, which delivers the passions from carnal grossness and limitation, also raises them beyond reach of fluctuation and inconstancy, attributes that are essentially those of the senses. However pure the thrill of passion, at the dawn of human love or a religious vocation, it is in too close proximity to the flesh and the ego; unpurified, there is a danger of its playing see-saw with love and exposing it to all the perils involved in "becoming". "The great and tragic illusion of loving souls," wrote Klages in one of his more despairing aphorisms, "is a belief that the force and depth of affection is any reliable guarantee of its permanence." The majority of human souls are in fact mausoleums, holding the ashes of spent passions that were once believed to have been created for eternity. Only those affections that are proof against breaking, that survive the "night" of their first component of sentiment—only such as these are destined to transcend time. A love is great and durable only as it profits by the sorrows and disappointments that come its way. . . .

We spoke, at the beginning of this chapter, of the human being's emotional unity and harmony. To this fulfilment every soul aspires. But there is only one way that leads to it, and it is one that nobody seeks: the narrow way, the way of the Cross. There is no myth more poisonous than the pretence that a universal synthesis of the affections can be realised at the level of sensible pleasure; this Utopia leads only to the dilution of all love and its ultimate death-agony. The synthesis of the passions and a transcendent love, of the joys of becoming and an eternal peace, can be accomplished only by anguish or the silencing of all that is sensible and temporal. But it is only a transitory extinction, and it is a fruitful one. The "night of the senses" of a John of the Cross is only a fleeting prelude, to be followed by an eternal resurrection of the senses. The dawn *begins* at midnight. In the dark depths of sensible dereliction, deliverance already appears in the spiritualised passions. He who would have man decline the Cross proves he knows nothing of man and nothing of the Cross. He proves, too, that he knows nothing of that profound affinity whereby fallen human nature and suffering are made so mysteriously complementary.[1] In this vocation of man to the Cross there is a necessity which—though accidental, in that it is the result of original sin—is *actually* as weighty as a necessity of nature, and quite as inevitable. As Scripture says decisively: "Man is born to suffer as a bird to fly."

[1] It may not be superfluous to point out that every utopian vision of humanity is inevitably accompanied by a horror of suffering. A notable defect in the obsolescent humanitarianism of our day is its ignoring what is vain and negative in man and also what is positive and fruitful in suffering.

CHAPTER III
Love and Marriage

THE CHOICE

I AM not offering any guidance in the art of choosing a mate, as some writers flatter themselves they can teach self-defence or even the art of making money on the Stock Exchange. I have no hard-and-fast recipes for practical use. Marriages, even those that are most carefully considered, must inevitably be conditioned by so many chances (those of fortune, circumstance, sentiment and opportunity) that it would be absurd to explore the ground armed with the rules of mathematics. Besides, human choice in the matter is so wrapped in obscurity that anyone who would choose too carefully, who is obsessed by any such notion as finding a "sister soul", runs a very grave risk of not marrying at all, or else of making some perfectly ridiculous choice, the kind of choice (to quote La Fontaine) "one would never have thought possible"—though we see it happening every day! "I have seen plenty of cautious buyers," remarked Friedrich Nietzsche, "but the canniest of them all bought his wife like a pig in a poke." A slight exaggeration, perhaps; but even in the most enlightened unions there is always an element of the leap in the dark, an element of gamble—the Pascalian *pari*. So the few general hints I propose to give should be regarded rather as probabilities than as certainties.

In the choice of a partner one of the most fundamental questions is obviously the biological one. To a very great extent it is on the health of the two parties that depend the moral and material equilibrium of the home, the existence and future of the children. But all I intend to do here is to consider the social and psychological aspects of the problem. Of the various contributing factors in the choosing of a mate there are some that are exterior or social (questions of background, class or fortune), others that are interior or psychological (dictated by love or reason). Let us stop for a moment to consider these two points.

THE SOCIAL BACKGROUND

Formerly this question never arose. Everyone married into his own class, and very often within the narrower bounds of his own parish or profession. The various social organisms, all solidly differentiated, never encroached on one another—though this, by the way, never involved an absence of interchange. Today, thanks to the ease and frequency of communications, and still more to the confusion of classes and functions, this state of things has completely changed. Unions are increasingly common between people of very different backgrounds, whether geographical, cultural or professional. In my own country, the Vivarais, to give only one example, a young peasant who in the old days would have married a girl of his own class, and not merely of his own class but of the inner circle of that class—belonging to a family with the same traditions as himself, the same political and religious opinions— unites himself now, as often as not, to a little typist from Paris or perhaps to some girl who has recently immigrated from Italy. Similar cases can be seen in every social class.

I would say quite frankly that such confusion is not by any means all to the good. In my view, identity of social *milieu* is one of the principal conditions of married happiness. Not that I would condemn all unions between persons of different environments; but I maintain they should be exceptional: they demand, from both parties, qualities of character one has no right to expect in the mass of people. When men and women, by marrying, enter a class higher than their own, or one merely different, they have to do so by *climbing*— there is a too prevalent notion today that one can get in anywhere "on ground-level"—and consequently they have to supply, by means of their capacity to love or adapt themselves, the common element that results naturally from identity of *milieu*. A marriage between a prince and a shepherdess never answers unless the shepherdess has the soul of a princess—a very rare occurrence. One of the failings of the modern world is to presume to make customary what should rightly be exceptional. It wants to make a general rule of what is superior to all rule; it thereby succeeds in falling *below* the general rule.

In a union between people of the same background, the whole complex of tastes and habits and common needs, all those imponderable biopsychological elements that come under the general appellation of *manners*, is a powerful contribution to the establishment of harmony. In the opposite case, the whole weight of their respective pasts tends in one way or another to separate the two parties. There is no gauging the extent to which material or moral behaviour, absolutely normal in a particular social *milieu*, may give rise to the gravest scandal and embarrassment in another.

An incident that actually occurred will illustrate this point. I happened to overhear one day a neighbour of mine, an old farm-woman, giving a lecture to her son. The lad wanted to marry the daughter of a shopkeeper in the village, but his mother refused her consent. "Don't take her," she warned him; and by way of an *ultima ratio* she added, in the tone of one denouncing an infamous crime: "She will want meat every day!" The rebuke was perfectly justified. In my part of the world, until the war before last, to have meat every day was wholly beyond the resources of the average worker; naturally, therefore, it was considered a culpable luxury, a species of vice. I admit I have chosen a glaring example; an extreme case, if you will. But it remains true that a married couple, with the best will in the world, are gravely liable to mutual misunderstandings and shocks due simply to their upbringing in socially different climates. This dead weight of custom, all the inevitable consequences of social background, it is well to have as an aid rather than as an obstacle to marriage. Great natures, I know, can overcome such handicaps; but I am speaking here for the average man. . . .

I may be told that mutual affection alone is enough to supply all these bonds of (what may be called) "climate"; that love, being all-powerful, has therefore all rights. But here I would plead for a little reflection. I know of no love that is all-powerful, except one: that spoken of by St John in his definition of God—*Deus est caritas*. I have always noticed, too, the very odd fact that the more a man claims for the absolute rights of love, the less his love is of the sort to work miracles and the more his "loves" seem to come to a bad end. . . . The love that is most powerless is that which is considered to consist solely of rights. An invitation, this, to inquire what it is that so often lies hidden beneath the fine-sounding title of "love". This brings us to the properly psychological factors that determine the choice of a partner.

LOVE OR REASON?

I hope I may be pardoned for digging up the old antithesis that present-day manners have succeeded in burying; but the very fact that it could have existed presents a problem and a challenge. Such dichotomies are the reverse of natural: they are the product of social and spiritual decadence. When we are confronted with a formula like this, the first thing we must usually ask ourselves, as a working hypothesis, is whether the words do not conceal a reality totally different from what they seem to express. Many surprising discoveries are to be made by this method. When a word is in fashion it will often be found that the thing it describes is actually very rare, or markedly obsolescent; people seize the idea as they would grasp at an alibi. As for the example we are concerned with here, if I had Chesterton's relish for the veracious paradox, I should say the most unreasonable of marriages is the so-called "marriage of reason", and the most selfish the alleged "marriage of love".

The defenders of the "rights of love" have been at pains to advertise (especially in the nineteenth century) the lamentable consequences imposed on two people when they marry for motives that have nothing to do with the attraction of the heart—considerations of class, fortune, circumstance and so on. All these social crimes were blamed on the "marriage of reason". Far be it from me to defend them. All I would say is that it is only necessary to look around to see that the "love-match", too, is very far from guaranteeing either harmony or stability.

I have taken the trouble to follow up, in my own part of the country, some typical cases of the "marriage of reason"[1] and also of the love-match.

---

[1] It would be truer to the facts, in such cases, to speak of a "marriage of *tradition*" rather than a "marriage of reason".

It was a matter, in the first instance, of young people marrying when they hardly knew one another. The circumstances, moral and material, of their respective families were almost identical. Our countryside abounds in well-meaning marriage-makers; all that was necessary was for one of these to get busy. In the second case, the young people married out of sheer mutual attraction, without family intermediaries, sometimes even in defiance of their families' wishes. What happened? Most of the "marriages of reason" produced healthy and sound homes; it was chiefly the so-called "love-marriages" that turned out badly, and this both from the personal and the family point of view: the results were voluntary sterility, misunderstandings, separations, and all the rest.

Reason and love are here really two violations of the unity of life, two separate and mutually contradictory idolatries.

I should like to make, at this point, a brief historical digression. In the classical epochs, institutions (whether moral, political or religious) transcended and supported the individuals who represented them. The monarchy was more than the king, the priesthood than the priest. The result was, one was free to criticise a particular king or pope without any calling in question of either the monarchical principle or the authority of the papacy. A saint like Catherine of Siena was unsparing in her attacks on the clergy of her day; a great Catholic like Dante could consign the reigning pontiff to hell! Today, as in every decadent age, we are witnessing precisely the opposite phenomenon. Institutions are tolerated or loved for the sake of the persons who stand for them. And that, incidentally, is why today more than ever we must have honesty and ability in our religious and political leaders. More than ever before, the leader who fails in his mission is disastrous: it is not only his ephemeral person he compromises but the enduring principle he is held to represent. It is an agonising sight to see feeble individuals having to bear on their shoulders the unrelieved burden of social institutions. Was it the principle of dictatorship to which Italians and Germans were yesterday so attached? Certainly not. What they worshipped were particular persons: Mussolini and Hitler. And can we imagine there could be an anti-clericalism today that would not be anti-religious at the same time? Alas, it is becoming more and more difficult to separate the cause of institutions from that of particular persons.

The institution of matrimony has naturally suffered from the same vicissitudes. In former times, persons were not merely subordinated to the institution, they were sacrificed to it. Under the old régime in France (and the same state of affairs existed in the nineteenth century in all social classes but the strictly proletarian) a girl vowed herself to marriage rather than to a particular husband. The person counted for little; the things that mattered were traditions and institutions. All this had its good side. In the first place, a union might have been contracted for reasons of social conformity, but there could be engrafted on it a sound and even passionate love. Again, even if such a marriage brought no personal fulfilment, husband and wife had at their disposal the institution itself, with its vast reserves of strength and continuity; they could draw, from this, the desire and courage to remain faithful to their duties. It is a characteristic of the classical "climate" to make the performance of duties and sacrifices spontaneous, so spontaneous as to be almost natural; such duties and sacrifices, in a decadent society, demand heroic feats from the individual personality. A wife of the *grand siècle*, in the hour of temptation, endeavoured to continue faithful to her husband, and also to something that vastly transcended him, to marriage itself. . . .

As long as such traditions remained living— drawing nourishment, that is, from their Christian sap and relying for strength on a personal God—they continued, in spite of the excesses inherent in everything human, to be very sound guides and organic supports to the individual. But as soon as they became severed from divine reality and forthwith degenerated into an anaemic formalism, they became burdens impossible for human nature to endure. Marriage, as it existed in certain bourgeois circles during the nineteenth century, refused a place in the sun to freedom and personality, to the ordinary man of flesh and blood. The "law" then demanded every sacrifice of man, and gave him in return none of the solid compensations that accompany all sacrifices of a religious character. Naturally the result was a

reaction. Personality then resumed its own place.
Its own? It acted like everything else that revolts
from constraint: it occupied the *whole* place! Hence a
reversal of all values: individuals had been sacrificed
to institutions; institutions were now to be sacrificed
to individuals. The rights of individual choice were
proclaimed absolute: everything must submit to the
arbitrary dictates of "love". Thus the nineteenth
century presented a curious spectacle: the dullest of
hide-bound conservatism side by side with a fever of
burning individualism. What the classical degenerates called order and law was merely the mask of
impotence and oppression; unfortunately, what
romantics of every description call love is more like
a highly flattering veil, something to throw over
glorified sensuality and selfishness. What is often
mistaken for true passion, for an act of profound
choice, is really something different: a very poor
mixture of instinctive attraction and pride. The
height of selfishness is a love-match that does not
spring from an intimate union of two souls but from
a craving for immediate and superficial happiness, a
happiness in which no sense of duty is involved. . . .
Hence the many miscalculations. Whoever marries
without consulting something else in himself than
what St Paul calls the lust of the eye and the pride of
life, has only to await satiety or the arising of a new
passion and he has a very good chance of hearing his
"voice of the heart" once again and of exercising
once more his alleged "right to love". It is hard to
be faithful to a choice that has been arrived at

arbitrarily, without any of those supra-personal influences that derive from moral and social environment.

The law, separated from God, and itself made a god, is nothing but an exasperating abstraction. But the concrete individual, equally separated from God and turned into a deity, becomes also an abstraction, something impotent and lifeless. We have to transcend this antithesis. The modern divorce of persons from institutions will result either in worse catastrophes still, or else in a new synthesis, finer and more exalted than any we have seen up to now. Institutions, it is conceivable, might be better adapted than hitherto to the needs and dignity of the individual person; persons might have more respect than they show today for recognised systems of society and morals.

Already the choice of a partner is ceasing, in many cases, to be guided solely either by "reason" or "love". It is becoming a "complete" choice: a choice made by love, but by a wider love, sufficiently enlightened to respect and include, together with the bodily or spiritual attractions of the individual, I won't say the prejudices, but the fundamental *exigencies* of life in society. Such a choice, I must add, must needs be impregnated with the religious spirit: it must be a choice relying on God, the creator alike of the individual and of society. Only in Him can all those elements be united which, under the essentially separating influence of idolatry, seem doomed irrevocably to perpetual war.

THE MARRIED STATE

After these somewhat extrinsic reflections, let us return to consider what may be properly called the married state itself. To be full and fruitful the union of husband and wife must rest on four things, which for purposes of discussion I will deal with separately, though in life they are closely connected, in fact virtually identical: passion, friendship, sacrifice and prayer.

Marriage and Sexual Life

"They will become one flesh", the Gospel says. My idea of marriage presupposes the existence of sexual attraction on both sides.

There are two rocks to avoid here; the absence of sexual attraction and the primacy of sexual attraction. Marriage should result in sexual fulfilment, but a fulfilment that is also a human fulfilment: that means it should rest on the attraction of the sexes, but an attraction that is possessed, crowned and transcended by the spirit.

There is a general tendency to underestimate what philosophers call material causality. Too long there has been a belief that conjugal union can exist independently of the rules of sex. Neither the fact of belonging to the same environment or class, nor mutual esteem, nor even a social or religious sense of duty, can be a substitute for a carnal passion that is not there. How many unions have foundered completely, or preserved no more than their legal

façade, for no other reason than sexual maladjust-
ment! The education of girls, it must be admitted,
as it has been conducted throughout the ages,
amounts to a paradox that even now arouses too
little astonishment. Children were brought up in a
mixture of ignorance and horror of the things of the
flesh; then without more ado they would be thrown
one day into an entirely new situation, where what
was yesterday always veiled as a sort of *mysterium
tremendum* must be abruptly accepted as a habit and
a duty. There is hardly any occasion to be surprised
after that at the total or partial failure of so many
unions, devised as they had been with total disregard
for the first exigencies of life.

But a union that is founded on sexual attraction
alone is no more truly a *human* union. Severed from
the roots, the stalk and flowers wither; but the root
also rots unless it is continued and controlled by
stalk and flowers. Nothing is so cheap, nothing so
empty beneath its outward glamour, nothing so
fragile, too, and vulnerable to time, as a love that is
dominated by sensual impulse.

Marriage, it has been said, is no solution to the
problem of sex. That is true, if the sexual problem is
regarded as something absolute, if the flesh is to be
glorified apart from the soul: this, in fact, is one of the
diseases of our time—sexolatry, the cult of the
bas-ventre. But it is false if sexuality is kept in its
place, if it is regarded not as an autonomous whole,
but as an organic part impregnated by the whole.
There are apostles of sex whose claims rest on a

confusion between sex and soul, between sex and God. For our part, we should desire no sexual fulfilment that must be bought at the price of human fulfilment; nor is the morality to our taste that would consummate sex by emptying man of his humanity. Marriage alone is capable of satisfying sex without any degradation of the person. . . .

This brings us to one of the best puffed-up bladders that contemporary psychology has ever contrived to inflate: the so-called "polygamous instinct of the masculine sex". I shall proceed to puncture it. Poor instinct, condemned to such unhappy repressions by matrimony! To start with, there is no such thing as a polygamous instinct. Instinct as such, in biological isolation and unadulterated by anything like spiritual infiltration, cannot possibly be said to be either polygamous or monogamous.[1] In regard to fidelity or change it is radically neuter; its place is altogether outside the range of these categories. . . . The sexual instinct of the animal is directed towards the female; whether she is the same or different is of no consequence at all. Very likely, if a new female appears, the male will desire her; but merely because she is a female, not because she is another one: he will be quite content with the same one he had yesterday, or the day before, or even the year before, provided she fulfils the required physiological conditions. The thing that impels man to polygamy

[1] I am speaking here for woman as well as man. If woman is more spontaneously faithful to one, that has nothing to do with her instinct as such, but to the integration—far more complete with her than with man—of her instinctive life with her love.

is *curiosity*, it is the sin of the spirit infiltrating into the instinct. Pure instinct desires another *qua* woman; sexual curiosity desires woman *qua* another. It is a very great mistake to think the sexual impulses of civilised man consist of nothing but sexual instinct; it is never possible to tell how much his instinct may be serving the will to power, the thirst to know or the craving to dominate. If this were not so, why should men show such zest in seducing women who, physiologically speaking, are very inferior to their own wives? When a man tries to be faithful to the woman he loves, it is not a case of the ideal being at war with instinct: there are two "ideals" in conflict, and the fight is mainly spiritual. The monogamous ideal wars with a kind of negative ideal, namely the sexual instinct impregnated and depraved by the appetite for change, the desire for knowledge or conquest; it fights against one of the many varieties of that false and devilish thirst for the infinite which has been consuming man ever since his original sin. The problem of conjugal fidelity is not physiological but moral. If the soul is simply and profoundly monogamous, the instinct can always be relied on to follow it. "If thy eye is clear", Christ said, "the whole of thy body will be lit up."

Conjugal fidelity, as we have said, is not the denying of the flesh for the sake of the soul, but the adoption and envelopment of the flesh by the soul. Here Nietzsche may well contribute the last word: 'In true love, it is the soul that envelops the body."

There is such a thing as matrimonial materialism:

it is marriage based on the pleasures of the flesh
alone. But there is also a pseudo-idealism in love.
This, though it condemns the flesh, is not itself
spiritual: it is a thing of dreams and compensations,
begotten of an impotent and perverse spirituality.[1]
These two disfigurings of love are equally to be
avoided. Complete realism should be the characteristic of the married state: a lofty Christian realism,
but one that includes the whole human being.
Husband and wife should endeavour to rise, not
like ascetics by denying the flesh, but (what is
perhaps more difficult) by drawing up the flesh in
the ascent of the soul.

Admittedly this arduous human ideal must
involve certain sacrifices in the sexual order. The
first of these sacrifices is the self-adaptation of each
to the sexual temperament of the other. In other
words, it must never be forgotten (as is sometimes
done by apostles of the imprescriptible rights of sex)
that the exercising of the sexual function, unlike that
of other instincts (nutrition, for example), necessarily
involves a partner. But the sexual constitution of a
woman, and to a proportionate degree her sexual
needs, are very different from those of a man. Apart
from this, account must be taken of individual
divergencies, due (for example) to temperament and

[1] There is no need to enlarge here on the subject of Platonic love.
It is normal enough at the age of puberty, and more common in the
case of girls than boys. When too prolonged or exclusive, it would
seem to be an inferior form of compensation. It should not normally
at any rate, exist in marriage. Conjugal chastity, and even continence, have nothing to do with this unrealist affectation and pseudo-
ideal.

education. If the enjoyment sought by each were only his or her own, what are we to suppose would be the result? An elementary sense of duty teaches husband and wife to make the pleasure received subordinate to that which is imparted. The maximum of *reciprocal* fulfilment is to be attained only through the partial sacrifice of *individual* fulfilment.

It may happen, too, that social, moral or biological necessities may impose a total sacrifice of carnal enjoyment. Such a sacrifice must be a true one, a frank and honest immolation, without subterfuge or rancour, or dubious compensations. In other words, it must be a sacrifice and not a repression. A true sacrifice, which immolates instinct, also sublimates and *transfigures* it; a repression, on the other hand, *transfers* and burlesques it, turns it into something sly and shameful, that flows back into the spirit and presently contaminates it: a source of resentment and false ideals and pharisaical virtues. Thanks to Nietzsche and Freud we need not elaborate the picture. . . . True sacrifice nourishes the soul; repression poisons it.

Much might be said of this sublimating of the instinct in married couples dedicated to continence, whether such continence be permanent or temporary. A study of the higher sexuality, in man and woman respectively, would be very illuminating in a connection such as this; but the subject is too vast and too delicate to approach here. It is enough to observe that in the strictly genital order man sublimates his instinct, as a rule, intellectually,

8

namely in an impersonal ideal; woman tends to sublimate hers in affection. If in the material exercise of sex woman is far less carnal than man, she is much more so in her healthiest sublimations of sex. Flesh and spirit, in her, interpenetrate to a degree never known in the opposite sex; into her most carnal emotions she puts far more soul than ever a man does; to make up for this, she mingles more, than he, of flesh with the passions of the spirit. It often happens that a woman is more affectionate the more she is deprived of complete sexual satisfaction: her sexuality, much less localised and brutish, much less animal than man's, finds almost adequate satisfaction in quite innocent endearments. Unfortunately, what in woman *replaces* full carnal possession, in man serves only to *incite* to such possession: instead of appeasing his instinct it merely lashes it the more. If women realised this, I believe continence in marriage would often be far easier.

Subordinated in this way to love and duty, bathed (as it were) in the spirit, bodily union is restored to its deepest significance and accomplishes its truly human finality. No longer a fleeting assuagement of two welded desires, the mere joining of two egotisms, it becomes the strongest possible expression of a mutual gift; the material seal of a union of souls, a sensible symbol of it. By virtue of this, corporal possession gives love a certain quality of achievement and irrevocability, known only to those who are truly husband and wife. It is sad that so many—

and many who are married—should profane this sacred emblem of love by offering the body and withholding the soul. Instead of coming first—and often, alas, alone—bodily union should come after the more precious gift, as its sequel and continuation: it should *descend* from love's fullness. So the branch casts its fruit, the heaven its dew.

The ultimate meaning of sexuality lies in the use man makes of it. Accordingly as it is *lived*, as it is employed by the personality, it can be the strongest manifestation of spiritual love, or it can be the worst of its obstacles. The sexual instinct can never operate in its simple animalism: it must rise above it or fall below it. Unless it climbs upward towards God it must drop down to the devil. If it is not *love* it becomes *lust*. It has often been suggested that a married couple (and especially the husband) may freely give rein to their lower impulses and commit carnal adultery while remaining faithful in soul. This is a hypocrite's defence of the worst kind of licence. As if the flesh were not impregnated, through and through, by the soul; and as if the soul were the *prisoner*, not the *form*, of the body!

Such a degree of spiritual integration of instinct is not, I know, either common or easy. I mention it as an ideal: one which those who are married should never lose sight of, whatever their actual frailties and shortcomings. If a life of mediocrity is bad in itself, consent to such a life is a sort of supreme evil, a sin against the spirit.

Marriage and Friendship

It is not on carnal passion that a pure and solid marriage can be built; nor is it—since man has no passions that are purely animal—on a superficial affection born of sexual emotion, nor on the sentimentality of romance or music-hall. The married state calls for communion very different from these, far more universal and profound. The love of husband and wife, if it is to be truly love and not a mere duping of the instincts, must be also a friendship.

Nietzsche wrote somewhere that every man, before embarking on marriage, should ask himself the question: Could I talk to that woman every day of my life? Certainly there could be no worse loneliness than to have as a partner for life a person with whom instinct was the sole means of communion. The flesh, as such, is not the gateway to the soul. Well might the poet write:

> Thy flesh impenetrable, because so near: stone, smooth and hard, that whets my solitude.
> That flesh of thine I touch can never enter into what is truly me.
> And all the while the farthest star in heaven steals through my eyes and down into my heart.

Paul Géraldy, too, in his little book *Toi et Moi*, has very well described that skin-deep affection with its purely sexual colouring that so many moderns mistake for love. "If you were a man," he makes his lover ask, "should we be friends?"

Sexual instinct, indeed, is nothing but isolation.
Animals seek one another out and copulate, but
psychologically they make no impression on each
other. A magnificent turkey-cock adorns my poultry-
yard. I often watch him at his antics as he clucks and
gobbles and struts hither and thither, using all his
sex-appeal, without the hen's condescending to pay
him the least attention; each bird has its own impenetrable existence, just like the windowless monads of
Leibniz; when they copulate it seems to be the result
of some pre-established harmony, not of anything like
sympathy in the psychological sense. A loneliness
like this, if it were possible to experience it, would be
the most insufferable and tragic of all conceivable
fates.

The sexual instinct is also a war. No kind of love
is so nearly akin to hate. Male brutality, female
artifice and coquetry, both alike bear witness to a
tension between the sexes. Naturally this tension has
been gravely aggravated and infected by the malice
of sinful man. When the *I* (in its bad, Pascalian
sense), with all its pride and will to power, is super-
imposed upon the sexual instinct, love can become
the most insidious of all wars. Even the attraction of
the "beloved" changes to torture and poison.
Psychologists who would have it that love between
man and woman is founded upon a mortal hatred
between the sexes have plenty of concrete arguments
to advance. What is the *femme fatale* of history,
woman the treacherous, the bringer of disaster—
Delilah, Cleopatra—if not a mingling of sexual instinct

with sin? She is a woman in whom there is engrafted on the flesh, not an exalting soul, but a corrupting ego.[1] Yet a true woman is first and foremost a soul.

Sexual instinct is also completely indifferent to personality. It seeks in the partner its own satisfaction, not the one and only being who is capable of satisfying it. As Géraldy asks again: "Would you love me much less if I were someone else?" Neither more nor less, as far as the instinct is concerned. As we have seen already, fidelity and change are wholly irrelevant to it.

Friendship, on the other hand, is something that penetrates the loved object, lives by its life and becomes wedded to its soul. Thereby it destroys that inner loneliness, the curse of all who have been brought together by instinct alone.

And friendship brings peace. It corrects and masters the tension that is inherent in the sexual dualism. Its function in sexual love is to preserve its original ardour and mend any differences that subsequently arise. It teaches man control over all that is violent and excessive in his masculinity; it teaches woman how to give without meanness or deception. And here is a particular point to note. To overcome sexual inconstancy and conflict, man possesses nothing but spiritual love; but woman,

---

[1] It is a tragic fact, and one that proves how much sex has been corrupted in humanity, that this is the only kind of woman that many can love. Their passion feeds on contempt and deception; it flags as soon as they are sure of being loved. Many a woman has lost the love of husband or lover through giving too clear proofs of her affection and fidelity.

apart altogether from spiritual love, has another instinct as well; this instinct, mingled as it is with her sexuality, gives her a depth and stability that are not in her own nature: what I am referring to is the highest and purest instinct of any, the greatest of all biological marvels—the maternal instinct. Woman, in fact, can achieve the wonder (not known perfectly in the animal world) of causing her sexual and maternal instincts to converge upon the same being. I believe it is no exaggeration to say that the firstborn of every woman who is naturally a mother is her husband. . . . That, I think, is one of the deepest reasons why a great love in woman is unaffected by time.

Finally friendship, the result of *personal* attraction and choice, gives the personality its proper place in love; it substitutes, for the *liaison*, necessarily ephemeral, between two egotisms, a stable *unity* of two beings, each chosen by the other and neither of them replaceable.

Friendship alone makes it possible for husband and wife to *understand* one another. Yet this friendship, however spiritual, remains somehow rooted in their sexual constitutions, and therefore in the *difference* between their sexual constitutions; hence, on one side and the other, it is bound to clothe itself in very different forms. To understand one another better— and to that extent to love better—husband and wife should understand before all else what is the *kind* of love with which the other loves. A love misunderstood may hurt or weary even more than indifference.

According to the *Nineteenth-Century Larousse* (under the article *Woman*) the most outstanding feminine trait is egotism. On the other hand women, as everyone knows, are for ever groaning over masculine egotism. Egotism, actually, is common to both sexes; but men differ from women in the form of their egotism, just as they do in the form of their love.

We know very well—and there is no need to stress what has been dealt with so often—the objects of a woman's love are, I won't say more concrete, but generally more immediate than a man's, more material, if you will. A woman's ideal is more "incarnate" than that of a man. Woman sacrifices herself naturally to those who are about her, to those whom she knows, in order to safeguard the immediate future of the race. Man, on the other hand, devotes himself rather to a universal good; his mission is to spend himself—often to exhaust himself completely—for ends that are probably no less real, but much more remote in space and time. The foundations are the province of the woman, the superstructure is the man's. Except, I think, in a few exceptional cases, no good is achieved by transposing the two functions. The public conscience tends naturally to count it a failing, if not downright lack of spirit, when a man gives up his mission in the state for the sake of a woman. The recent abdication of a King of England is a case in point. But given the same choice, a woman who would give up the man she loves simply for the sake of playing at politics or philosophy would incur very rightly the charge of being ridiculous.[1] Heroism, in the two sexes, is very differently polarised. . . . So too is egotism: I mean the normal and good egotism. That of a woman consists in withdrawing from the distant and universal in order to devote herself better to the things that are at hand; that of a man is rather to neglect the immediate for the sake of pursuing some loftier and more distant good. This divergence is apt to have embarrassing consequences. A husband, for instance, waxing really enthusiastic about his pet ideas, is a little disconcerted when his wife interrupts: "By the way, what about dinner? Suppose I make a cheese soufflé. . . ." Conversely, of course, women are often astonished at the lack of consideration and attention shown by the male in a thousand little circumstances of ordinary daily life. In such cases the only safeguard against resentment is understanding: remembering it is possible to be loved just as much as one loves, and even more—but not with the *same* love. In practice, a reciprocity of love between husband and wife always begets a certain identity of love. The love of a wife grows more universal as it comes in contact with her husband's ideal; similarly the love of a man shows more practical consideration under the mellowing influence of a woman's affection. The married state performs for both the greatest possible service that any limited and one-sided being can receive: salvation from self. . . .

[1] Someone may object here that religious vocations are common enough among women. But this is wholly different. A woman who gives up her mission among those she loves, in order to give herself to God, sees this God as a person, the most intimate and actual *You*.

There is another essential difference in the structure of their respective loves. The affection of a woman is infinitely less dependent on the intellect than is man's. A woman's heart is somehow autonomous. A man loves a woman for her qualities. He has, or thinks he has, reasons for loving her: he justifies his love at the judgement-seat of conscience. A woman, on the other hand, loves a man for himself; with her, love alone suffices for love; reasons for loving are confused with love itself. A man will say: I love you because you are beautiful, or gentle, or good. The woman will say simply: I love you because I do! For man, to love a woman is to prefer her. For woman, to love is—to make no comparisons. A subtle distinction. . . .

It is a common saying that love in woman is more "blind" than in man. What is less often noticed is that feminine love, for the very reason that it is blind *qua* love, because it relies very little on reasons for loving, is much more clear-sighted in regard to the object of its affections. It feeds less on illusions. The less love is dependent on the intellect, the freer the intellect to function independently of love. And this is just what happens in woman. A man's love is a thing of judgements and comparisons; whenever it feels itself menaced by some lack in the person loved, it has a way of promptly reacting with illusions. Woman, on the other hand, can see right through the man she loves without the least detriment to her love itself. She has no need to be blind to her husband's shortcomings. Beyond the banal and more or less interchangeable qualities that are often the motives for masculine love, hers can penetrate (as it were) to the unique and indestructible substance; it takes a place, quite naturally, behind all deception where it needs no support of make-believe or illusion. A woman can be in love with some man, and consumed with admiration for him, yet be perfectly aware of all his weaknesses. Hence a man can always reveal himself to a woman as he is; he can descend to all that is lowest in his nature without in the least endangering her love. The case of wives of criminals is typical in this respect. I think too many men, measuring women by themselves, think there is only one way to win or keep their affections: that is by disguising their own failings and striking impressive attitudes in the hope of being able to throw dust in their eyes. In this way they succeed, not in increasing the woman's love (which never stood in need of such pretences anyhow), but rather in exciting her ridicule. Hence Toulet's remark: "Women know very well men are not as stupid as they are commonly thought—but far stupider. . . ."

If it is the flesh that brings man and woman together, it is only friendship that can reveal them to each other as they are. At the same time—and what we have said already shows this clearly enough—that perfect intellectual "transparency", the principal charm of friendships between men, is something theirs can rarely attain. The two sexes are complementary, and therefore different; each remains somewhat opaque to the other. More than this, the love that unites them actually lives on this mutual mystery; it depends, to some extent, on the fact that complete "understanding" is impossible. What attracts us in a friend is what we know of him; in a woman it is what we don't know. As a proof of this, whereas friendship grows stronger, the deeper we penetrate the soul of a friend, love (as Proust observed) often diminishes as we strip a woman of her mystery. We have to acquiesce in this state of affairs. The reason, I think, why many husbands are disappointed lies in the fact that their love is too intellectually exacting. A wife, they would have it, should be possessed as much by the mind as by the heart. But we could never love a woman we understood to that extent, because she would no longer be a woman, she would not be the strange being who serves to complete us. One might adapt Géraldy's question, and ask our dearest friend: "If you were a woman, should we be lovers?" In marriage, as in the mystical life—I have no wish to push the analogy too far, but it exists—it is necessary to respect and love what is not fully understood. The love of the creature, also, calls for acts of faith.

Marriage and Sacrifice

If there is a tragically urgent task awaiting the moralist of today, it is surely that of recalling mankind to the idea of sacrifice. It is to losing sight of this necessity that all failure and wretchedness in marriage is due. Surely without mutual sacrifice no marriage can be happy. This is not a paradox. The first condition of happiness is that it should never be sought. Here one might misquote the Gospel and say: Seek not and you shall find.

A man of any nobility of character is principally concerned to live as a man: the baser types of humanity are content to live happily. The aim of the latter, in this world, is to find the things and persons that give them satisfaction; the former seeks those for whom he can sacrifice himself. He *gives himself* to a wife, he does not take her. To surrender possession of the self there is no means more exclusive or direct than marriage. "Everyone who marries should remember he is losing fifty per cent of his independence." Coming across this in an American paper, G. K. Chesterton made the comment that such optimism would be permissible only in the New World!

The secret of married happiness is to have a love for this dependence. It is the cost, not the value received, that should measure the degree of conjugal love.

The vocation of marriage is also a consecration. This explains much. It gives meaning to all the duties and all the sorrows of the married state. Above all it makes conjugal fidelity no longer a kind of barren sacrifice but a religious act of supreme human value.

Inability to be faithful is primarily due to an inability to make sacrifices. For so many men the

motive of love is immediate pleasure. . . . This
prevents their ever knowing more than the surface of
what they love; as soon as the surface deceives them
they abandon it altogether, and this they continue
to do indefinitely. To skim everything and go to
the heart of nothing, such is what many proclaim
to be freedom and fulfilment. Running is so much
easier than digging. But he who would plumb the
depths of any creature must first learn the way to
suffer for that creature. His love must surmount
disappointment and habit; not only so, but it must
learn to feed on disappointment and habit. Human
love has its own aridities and nights; it, too, has to
find its true centre by way of suffering and defeat.
But having reached that centre it enjoys for ever all
the treasures of the creature for whom the sacrifice
was made. Superficially the creature may be
appallingly limited, but its depth is infinite as God's.
Poets have always sung this love that, by way of
something fleeting, can seize upon the eternal:

> You who pass away and fade,
> Beyond the days, beyond the skies, I sought for you,
> Upon the everlasting will's eternal shores . . .
> Down into the lowest depths I sought,
> Beneath the beating of your heart,
> Below the wellspring of your vows,
> Into that solemn centre wherein your life to Life is
>   tied,
> Into the quivering depths of the unchanging,
> Into the throbbing mystery of God's creation!
>   —It is your soul I love!

In married life, admittedly, there is much that is humdrum and monotonous, much that is of the earth earthy. I know all too well how capable man is of vulgarising and prostituting whatever is most profound. But if married life is often dull, what epithet are we to apply to sexual life outside marriage? It is one of the cleverest of the devil's tricks to try to persuade mankind that order means death, disorder life. In reality nothing is duller than vice. The devil is not deep: he is merely a rebel, a deserter who wants to be taken for a refugee. . . .

The humble realities of daily life, the procession of little duties and sorrows, should make no difference to the purity of married love. The true ideal draws its sap from these little things. The realism of married life should not mean the profaning or exhausting of the first ideal; its function is to purge it of its illusions, but to preserve all that is finest in it. In any husband and wife who are worthy of the name, the union of the highest form of love with the most material of earthly necessities makes for a kind of synthesis of the ideal and the real, I might say a realising of the ideal, impossible anywhere else in a similar degree.

Joséphin Soulary said of God: "If he were only in heaven he would be nowhere." Marriage is the vocation above all others in which it is possible to see God in the things that are outwardly most trivial and commonplace.

And here is something very important I nearly forgot. Marriage should be a sacrifice, admittedly, but a mutual sacrifice. Nothing could be vainer or

more harmful than a one-sided sacrifice. Two
egotisms coupled together tend to curb one another
and somehow cancel each other out. But what a
hotbed of egotism is life in an atmosphere of untiring
devotion! We have all seen homes where the sacrifices of either husband or wife have turned the other
into a monster of exacting selfishness. The partner's
generosity should not be a *pretext* for living at ease; it
should rather be a *motive* for vying in self-sacrifice.

Love and Prayer

Self-sacrifice for another, loving the other in spite
of his worthlessness, even because of his worthlessness, with a love stronger and purer than any desire
for happiness—this is something not possible unless
human love is intimately united with eternal love.

It is not a matter of making a god of the person
loved. An idolatry of this sort leads quickly enough
to indifference or even revulsion. True married
love accepts the beloved, not as a god, but as a gift
from God, a gift in which God himself is included.
Such a gift as this there is no confusing with God.
And there is no separating it from God.

"She was looking upwards, and I at her," wrote
Dante of Beatrice. This is the great secret of human
love: to drink in the divine purity of it in the gaze of
the eyes, in the soul, in the gift of a creature.

Feel sacred Being throb within the being loved. . . .

Such is Hugo's fine definition of true love. The
beloved, thus loved, is really irreplaceable: as the gift

of God, the beloved is unique like God, the dwelling of an inexhaustible mystery. Those who are truly husband and wife are lovers for ever; possession, for them, is merely a profounder virginity. The more they are all in all one to another, the more they crave to remain so. There is a manner of possessing things —and it is something sacred—which instead of killing the desire, like carnal satisfaction, actually exalts and transfigures it. "Anyone who drinks such water as this will be thirsty again afterwards. . . ." How can it cease, the love of husband and wife, when they have been created and joined together in order to give one another God? In a single prayer their wedded life unfolds, and in that prayer it grows immortal.

CHAPTER IV

The Purifying of Love

LIKE the colouring of daily life or artistic creation, like divine love itself, the love of creatures involves phases of aridity, alternating periods of illumination and darkness. Here too there is a desert that has to be traversed before there is any entering into the Promised Land.

We have said "the love of creatures". It is a vast subject, and we shall restrict ourselves here to what is properly called "love": that is, the love of the sexes, the closest bond that can exist between two creatures in this world.

The decision can be justified on two grounds. We shall avoid generalising too much if we limit and confine the subject under discussion. And apart from this, what we observe in sexual life—using the term in its widest sense—is, from our present standpoint, especially significant. It is obvious that all love between creatures—whether it be maternal love or filial, friendship or admiration—may undergo periods of arid purification; but such alternations of light and shadow are most frequent and intense in sexual love. None other runs so stormy a course, rises to such heights or descends to such depths.

Why this unhappy privilege? Why these bitter cycles in the love of man and woman, when the affection of a mother for her son, of friend for friend, normally develops without any such shocks or depressions? It is here we touch the basic dualism of sexual love.

There is no suggestion that sentiments such as friendship, or maternal or filial love, are not susceptible to progress or purification; all that is claimed is that these affections are from the outset on a far higher level of biospiritual harmony, that they have a higher degree of loyalty and personal attachment, than those associated with the beginnings of sexual love. In the former affections, the instinctive and sensuous components contrive naturally to adjust themselves to the spiritual element. But the love of the sexes is rooted in those animal depths that are almost autonomous, at any rate alarmingly impenetrable by the spirit. Biologically, sexual attraction is the most inconstant of passions, the least attached to its object *as a person*. In sexuality pure and simple, the partner is only an ephemeral and subordinate *means*.

Yet, in the spiritual and personal order, no love takes such a strong and complete hold as the sexual. Nothing among all created things—as every lover feels when love first awakens—implies a greater demand for the absolute and eternal than this passion that emerges from the hidden impulse of the flesh; nothing is so calculated to unite and fulfil his personality as this flame of sex, the very nature of which seems merely to serve a non-personal end.

The paradox of love lies in just this incongruity

between the animal roots and the spiritual flower; it lies still more in the obliterating of the incongruity by the reabsorbing of the root by the flower. It is the miracle of true human love that it can use the force of sexuality, basically alien and centrifugal to the final destiny of the soul, to nourish all that is most delicate in the interior life. Therefore, to bridge the abyss between the biological reality of love and what it may become in the human soul, there is need for a severe ordeal of purification.

THE BIRTH OF LOVE

True love between man and woman does not begin in the flesh to end in the soul. Both at its origin and at its goal there is an inevitable intermingling of soul and body. The whole being is affected. Love's progress is rather from the flesh, impregnating, guiding and steeping the soul, to the soul, impregnating and guiding the flesh. It starts with a dream of human fulfilment and ends in its reality.

Love begins, as we have said, with the soul's being surprised, almost ensnared, by the flesh. One could say it begins with an illusion. Not that this is peculiar to love. Everything great, in this world, begins with a dream. So it has been written: Woe to him who has never dreamed. There is no climbing to heaven without passing through clouds. The presence, the mere image of the loved one, is experienced as something new, something mysterious and ravishing. As by sudden magic, the old self is

banished and the soul is filled with the raptures of
the blessed. A frail creature appears in our path,
and now all is changed for us. This creature hence-
forth lives at the centre of our being, at the centre of
the world. She is inexpressibly *unique*, "something
that can never appear twice". By her, our inner
world is transfigured; she awakens, in our depths,
powers never before suspected; we seem to receive
our very soul at her hands. "The fountain from the
which my current runs," exclaims Othello. And the
whole outer universe, through her, assumes an
aspect virginal, sublime. Hear how the poets
proclaim this strange transformation:

> The spark has tasted of the fire, for me thy lips have
> tasted of the world . . . and the words that fell from
> them have taught me the immemorial ways that
> mount up into the heart of things . . .
> From thee flows forth the honey and the dawn, the
> starry harvests, the transfiguring ray . . .
> A tear fell from thy eye, and mirrored in that tear I
> saw the world. And the foundations of the world
> lay open to me. In thy eyes my gaze is drowned . . .
> See how all creation throbs, clad in the wealth of some
> primordial glory.
> Thy eyes unlock those ancient rusty chains of weari-
> ness and death; all is secrecy, suspense, and the
> very stones upon the way weep maiden's tears.
> The universe is a treasure-trove beneath thy lids.

More than anything else in the world, the rapture
of a new-born love gives man the illusion of discovering a paradise on earth.

But this rapture, that promises all and sometimes even appears to give all, is a thing that has to be scrutinised more closely.

Strangely enough, though it communicates an inward warmth to the soul and a lyrical pleasure of unspeakable intensity, it involves no sense of inner purification, no "conversion" in the deeper sense of the word. It changes the colouring of the emotions but not their orientation. Morally, love adds nothing to the stature of the lover. It effects a revolution in the *sensations* of the man that was; it makes no difference to his aims or interests, or to his general attitude to himself and the world at large. Admiration, friendship, even maternal love can produce no satisfaction without at least a minimum of purifying and self-denial. But the joy that results from sexual love is independent of any spiritual uplifting of the individual. No one has ever observed this fulfilment, brought about in the soul by the exhilaration of a great passion, make any change in a lover's egotism or ambition or ill-temper. It will be lucky (as we shall see later) if it does not aggravate his failings.

At first sight the rapture of a new love seems to spring from the depths of the soul, from the immortal centre of the personality. But really its source is much lower. Primarily it springs from instinct and the ego: the two forces which, when ill controlled, so easily turn to parasites and become the sepulchre of the soul.

Beneath this airy tenderness, beneath these rays

of purity that envelop first love, there lurks, concealed but implacable, the blind urge of instinct and the species. When lovers declare they love with all their soul, when they solemnly swear they will be faithful for ever, there is no reason to doubt they are speaking from the depths of their being. But the cosmic impulse beguiles and abuses their spiritual personality; the flesh (as it were) has their soul in tow, and what they call love may well be mere glamour, the instinct's feelers and *pretext*. First love, it is true, consists of more than the merely sensuous and ephemeral. How else could one account for its thirst for the absolute, its spontaneous faith in the one chosen from among all? But it attains the spiritual and eternal only by way, and through the *agency*, of the sensuous and ephemeral. It is not "soulless"; but the soul in it is seduced, as it were bewitched from without. It imbues the whole human personality, but its well-spring lies in the sub-human depths. This is proved clearly enough by all the loves that wither when the carnal and romantic appeal begins to fade.

Another rock lies ahead. The ego—I mean by this all those potent and subtle forces of narcissism and self-idolatry—has a way of battening on the pleasures and plenitude of love. The experience of persons and epochs, the witness of moralists and writers of fiction, show how much "love" and pride are intermingled in the sex relationship. Pride of possession and mastery in man, pride in being desired and chosen in woman: these emotions are so strong that many psychologists have held that this is all there is in love; simply the duel of two egotisms. Even in couples who escape this conflict, the ego retains all its rights: in these, love gives birth to a kind of complacent well-being, a double egotism, as deceptive and vain as individual egotism. In short the ferment of love has no purifying effect; it merely enlarges what it finds. Where egotism and vanity are reigning already, it magnifies egotism and vanity.

First love develops in the form of an idolatry. Not that this is due to an excessive love for the partner; quite the contrary. *The only idol is the self:* the myth of Narcissus is the unique and eternal symbol of idolatry. Here the object of man's worship is his own desire, the exaltation of himself. The rôle of the beloved is merely secondary, that of being the source and condition of the lover's pleasure. The result is, the lovers never enter into each other's true being; they never really know each other. What they love in one another is not the eternal substance of being, but a phantom they create in the image of their own desire. Sexual love, before it is purified, is a kind of parody—a monstrously egotistical parody—of the creative act of God. Fed by the instinct and the ego, the two forces that are essentially in rebellion against all communion and openness of heart, a love of this sort remains radically subjective. It does nothing to destroy the selfish isolation of the individual; for all the enthusiasm it arouses, there is nothing liberating in it. A bird may fly swift and

far without acquiring possession of space; it knows
no freedom as long as it worships its own flight.
On the other hand, a bird in captivity, accepting
the limitations of its cage, is free; it is in inward
communion with the universe all about it. Of all the
concrete signs of narcissism in love, one of the most
characteristic is an almost constant irritability, a
spirit of suspicion, quarrelling and jealousy. The
lover who is peevish and overbearing because his
partner fails to conform to a servile reflection of
himself, shows clearly that his love is fundamentally
selfish.

THE CRISIS OF LOVE

Bound up as it is with all that is material and
tainted in human nature, the fruition of first love is
essentially precarious. Neither the fleeting and
perishable flesh nor the self-enclosed ego, always
hungering for novelty because nothing can appease
it, is any fit basis for a really firm and constant
affection. It is not in self-seeking that man's supreme
reality consists, but in open communion with the
beloved. Love in its earliest stages is unrealistic, and
therefore quick to wither up when it comes into
contact with realities. Illusion is a hot-house plant.
. . . So it is that man enters on the second phase of
love: the discovery of the void.

There are many things that may destroy love's
spontaneous rapture. There are a thousand doors
by which disillusionment may enter the soul. Daily
intercourse stales and withers the loved one's charms;

it brings out, too, all the imperfections and shortcomings. That is what may happen when, through
some material or moral necessity, love is deprived of
carnal pleasure and undergoes a stage of aridity and
frustration. Sometimes, too, things take the opposite
course: the same joys of the flesh, coarsened and
robbed of significance by use and habit, lose that
halo of immaterial purity and no longer draw the
soul in their train. Or again a new love may invade
the heart, usurping and monopolising the forces
of desire and so causing the original affection to
fade. In all these cases the fullness of affection is
replaced by dryness and love itself is plunged into
the dark.

Then comes the bitter feeling of having sunk into
a veritable pit of inanition, of having descended to
the very negation of love. The lover seems to have
plumbed the depths of the beloved. But in reality it
is merely his own depths he has plumbed, the
depths of his self-enclosed ego and fugitive instinct;
and since he was never made to live by himself the
rapture of his love, deprived of air, flickers out,
leaving nothing behind but its barren ashes. But
he who falls back so heavily upon himself has never
really emerged from himself; his love has never
passed the narcissist stage; the trial he has undergone
—simply contact with reality—gives him back his
essential poverty and insufficiency. The disillusioned
lover, who fancies he has exhausted the object
of his love, has often barely touched the surface of
that love: what he has struck is not the bedrock of a

soul—souls have no bedrocks—but his own limitations, his own real impotence. When a pair of lovers are mutually disillusioned, it is almost certain that what each had loved in the other was nothing else but the self. The disappointment comes, not from the other, but from the self, from the false orientation of their love, from its straying into the *impasse* of self-seeking. A soul is capable of penetrating another: all an ego can do is to clash with itself. Disillusionment is the result of the ensuing shock. . . .

At this moment of crisis when, after its brief deluding glitter, all the meanness and frailty of a love stand revealed, it is easy to be harsh and ungenerous to the loved object. It is a natural reaction in a lover to hold the other responsible for all the pains and disappointments arising from the failure of their love. This explains why some married couples, who have enjoyed the carnal and material fulfilment of their love, reveal a kind of "unexplained hatred"; this is the tortured relic of what was once a true love, trampled in the dirt by habit, by the dead joys of the flesh that the soul has long deserted.

Here is a poet's painting of this voyage across the abyss, the crisis in which outcast love grows doubtful of its own existence:

> Dear child, a thorn embedded in my heart,
> The heart you pierce without possessing,
> I would cry: I love you, with the voice of fragrant
>   flowers and streams,
> With the voice of all the fleeting things that perish to
>   themselves . . .

But I—I am not fleeting, neither do I die, and the
ever-busy needle of my pain, the needle of your
image too beloved, knits close the stifling solitude
about me, knits the yearning expectation,
anguish of a present that can never pass away—
A present, stretching out unwearied arms towards a
future empty of content . . .
Dear child—not God . . .

Or again:

You might never have been. You might never have
been for me. What faint and futile chance,
chance self-ashamed, was it that wed our ways;
what colourless dull dawn transformed eternity
for me . . .
Why are you called "All and Always", beneath
whose aureole, beneath whose fatal lure, there
lurks the stench of accident, remoteness, nothingness?
Why should you, centre to nothing, be my centre? . . .
You gave me all—save but the power to take! Your
freshness was a fire consuming me. Why had it
not been yours to recreate my soul after the
image of my own desire, to make of me *another*
that would still be I? I hated as I loved you—for
me the very taste of love was changed!
I saw your love grow dimmer, like a lamp withdrawn. The days we passed together are now
yesterdays, diminishing, receding yesterdays. In
your embrace I stifle, desiring to escape the
place no longer lit but darkened by your eyes.

A tragic testing, to find oneself alone and empty,
even if it is not consciously experienced as tragic but

merely as a fading into the greyness of succeeding days; a trial made all the lonelier and more empty by those early dreams of communion and fulfilment! It is a time of ingratitude, not only to the one who had been loved but to love itself. Reduced to a state of inward isolation a man sees love as a mere projection of himself, the play of something purely subjective:

> All I loved in thee was my own rapture.
> *(Bouilhet)*
> It is the self we seek in thinking to escape it.
> *(Anna de Noailles)*
> Love is like a Spanish inn: you find there what you bring. *(Mérimée)*

This arid phase gives rise even to doubts as to whether there have been two different people involved: the very reality of the *object* is questioned. You have only to analyse the disillusionment—and God knows the moderns have not been failing in this—to get the impression that love is not an offering, an opening of the heart, but a process of conquest and annexation, or even a veiled form of that desiccating *libido sciendi*. To love is to covet the secret of a being, not to share it but to slay it; it is a shameless scrutinising of the inward parts of a being; it is an absorbing into oneself, a *taking*, and thereby a dooming the thing taken to sterility. For man receives only in the measure that he gives; it is only the being to whom he offers himself that he truly possesses. In love, all that is gained by conquest is what is already dead.

For lovers like these, love is measured by curiosity, the morbid attraction of mystery. I say morbid, because it is one thing to love the mystery of a creature in order to plunge deep into that mystery and live by it; another, to love the mystery for the sake of tearing it out and casting it to the winds. The latter sort of love perishes when curiosity is satisfied. The loved being is not ground to cultivate and live on, not a *native land*, but rather a territory to explore, a holiday resort to look at and forget . . . "He will love you", says Marie Noël:

> To make a voyage of discovery . . .
> But once he captures every untamed bird
> That sings within the bower of your heart,
> What nightingale have you to take him word
> That he return to you ere day depart?

Proust, too, describes very well this sterile craving to know everything, to transfix all with that mortal curiosity that causes a child to eviscerate its doll, the miser to kill the goose that lays him the golden eggs, that unholy thirst for the fruit of the tree of knowledge that robs men of the fruit of the tree of life: "We love a woman to strip her of her mystery."

This dryness of affection, the sensuous eclipse of love, may develop in three directions.

First, towards the death, pure and simple, of love. Many are the "eternal" passions that need but a few moments of time to be cast into oblivion.

Alternatively, towards a symbiosis of egotisms, an artificial compromise between two souls grown strangers, utterly closed one to the other:

> Live thy tedium at my side,
> I, beside thee, will nurse my loneliness.

A more or less mechanical affection may still keep such dead unions in being, but the continued association will depend chiefly on a sharing of carnal satisfaction, on material interest or social convention. Husband and wife serve as mutual supports; it is just acquired momentum that keeps them together. . . . The frequency of these precarious and artificial unions has provided a pretext in every age for the immoralist's facile criticisms of marriage.

Or finally, the testing may result in the deepening and transfiguring of love.

THE TRANSFIGURING OF LOVE

In those living in religion it is possible to distinguish two very different kinds of aridity: the performance of acts of piety may engender dryness, either through a process of supernatural purification, or through lack of fervour and attachment to the things of the world. It is the same with profane love: the "nights" which are an introduction to a clearer and sublimer love should not be confused with the kind of aridity that precedes the complete extinction of all love. There is a dryness that ripens and a dryness that kills. In the first case love feels numbed and bewildered, but painfully alive beneath the ordeal of its testing; in the second there is just an unfelt painless detachment. But the importance of this distinction should not be exaggerated. We are not on the mystical plane here. We believe the outcome of these "nights" of human love depends on the attitude a man adopts to them and the use he makes of them. The same aridity that when surmounted leads to the transfiguring of love, when accepted meanly and selfishly brings love to the grave.

Intimacy is the great test of love. Sexual passion becomes atrophied by habit or else frustrated, either through loss of health or other vital exigencies, or through unavoidable sacrifices. On the other hand, the slow discovery of the *reality* of the loved being destroys little by little the inner idol of the loved one, the idol that was none other than the *idealised projection of the self*, the image of what the lover himself lacked. The discovery of *the other* is a bitter experience for narcissist idolatry. . . .

Love is then at the crossroads. The flesh and the ego can no longer find sustenance in the loved being. There must be an intervention of the soul in all its depth and purity; otherwise love dies. It is the moment for heroism, for a holy war—in love, the only true and lawful war—in which man must arm himself, not to conquer another but to defend the gift he has made of himself; it is the moment for *believing* in the loved one, in spite of disillusionment, in spite of the rapture that is dead; it is the moment that proclaims to lovers, whatever the illusions and

baser elements in their love: Even now there is time
to save from perishing that germ of eternity in your
love when it was new.

Whoever continues to love in spite of disillusionment succeeds at last in loving the object for itself.
There then occurs a kind of reversal of feeling: to
the gross subjectivity of first love there succeeds a
complete loss of self. The lover learns the reality of
love; he feels himself bound to the other, overcome
by the other, overpowered by a strange destiny.
And he experiences a new joy: the solemn joy of
self-surrender, silent and imperishable. Moreover,
what he loves now is the very poverty of the beloved.
The poorer the creature the more he has to give.
His love is now chaste and tender; he would offer
himself wholly to the loved one without making the
smallest demand in return. It is something far
higher than mere exchange, than the *do ut des;* it even
thrives on disillusionment.

But it is true here also that he who is willing to lose
his life will receive it back again immortal. He who
has given all is in a condition to receive all. Loved in
so disinterested a way, the creature is an inexhaustible source of delight. In the hour of dryness the
lover believed he had touched the bedrock of his
love, but all he had reached was the bedrock of his
desire, the bedrock of his idol. But idols are not
deep. Now, for the first time, he discovers the soul
of the beloved. Purified by trial, by his fidelity amid
the ruin of all that was narrow and base in his love,
he at last finds himself capable of communion with

that soul. It is now infinitely liberating to him, infinitely transparent. He was able to love the emptiness of it, and now the void is peopled with wonderful blessings, like a deserted region suddenly invaded by light. For it is only to hearts free from concupiscence that creatures ever reveal their authentic treasures; they never offer what is deep and eternal in their being except to him who has loved them first for everything they lacked.

There is nothing in the world so pure and satisfying as this deliverance of sexual love. It is a resurrection: fresher, more tender, more virginal than birth itself; and it is clothed in eternity. Pleasure-love and vanity-love are now left behind. Man is no longer the tortured slave of his desire; he is the slave of a soul, and in such dependence finds peace and freedom. It is unspeakably serene, this affection that rises out of the void: it knows nothing of fears or doubts or jealousies. The lovers walk free from all the menaces of chance, bound together at the very source of their twin destinies, at the roots of being that neither lie nor die; an utter security envelops their love, which for them now merges into existence and necessity. Desire itself loses its note of want and restlessness; it is calm and brimming over: hunger becomes repletion, hope is barely distinguishable from possession. The soul at last understands the true nature of love, defined of old as a "going out from oneself" (*amor trahit amantem extra se*), the "wishing well" to another soul. It perfectly represents the meaning of those words that liberate while they bind: I love you.[1] Love, until now, had been no more than a thought; it was not till the trial was over that love's true countenance appeared. An awakening, this, not only truer but fairer than the dream. . . .

During this phase of illumination man realises, after all, how true was that presentiment of first love and its craving for the infinite. That pure fulfilment, dreamed of at the dawning of affection, treated as a phantom by souls that remain dis-illusioned, is recognised now as no less real than the dreary ashes of days gone by—indeed far more real, for it is from these very ashes that it draws its susten-ance. It is suffering that fulfils the promise of young love.

What is most important of all, at this crisis of love, is to know how to die in order to be born again. There must be no resisting the transformation effected by the trial. True fidelity consists in mastering and integrating this change, not in suppressing it. In the hours of dryness the most dangerous temptation to lovers is that of returning to the cradle of their affection. "Remember", says the troubadour, "how our love began." But spiritual, unlike cosmic, circles are not just simple repetitions of the past; every phase results in some-thing wholly new and unforeseeable.[2] The joy

[1] In Italian the natural way of expressing love is to say: *ti voglio bene* (I wish you well). I know nothing more moving than this popular expression of affection which corresponds perfectly with the metaphysical definition of love.

[2] On this subject it is worth reading Jean Guitton's valuable study of Rhythms ("*Les Rhythmes et la Vie*", *Editions du Groupe lyonnais*, pp 1–18).

that the trial engenders is not the same as that which was lost; it is *another* joy. An idolatrous regret for the dawning distorts and sterilises the purifying effects of the period of aridity. Whoever sighs for a happiness that has passed will discover, in the words of another troubadour, that "today's worth is always less than yesterday's". Our tomorrows must never be botched-up yesterdays, they must be yesterdays transfigured. There must be no clinging to old dreams; these must be allowed to die. Woe to him who has never dreamed, as we have said. But we could say more truly still: Woe to him who cannot die to his dreams. Like clouds on the horizon, dreams in the soul blur the clear definition of earth and heaven; when they disperse, they disclose once more what is truly earth and what is truly heaven. Dying to illusions does not involve any inhering in what is "of the earth earthy", no acquiescence in mediocrity; on the contrary, it makes possible a frank confronting of earth and heaven and a direct and harmonious unification of their realities.

The voyage of Columbus to America is a wonderful symbol of the transforming effects of love. First he turns his back on the east, on all the cradles of the dawn; without looking back he plunges into the realm of night, leaving behind all the things of childhood, only to find, at the farthest confines of the western ocean, an eternal orient, an unchanging dawn—and the *Pacific* Ocean. For if joy was the companion of love at its birth, *peace in joy* is to be found only after a painful pilgrimage. It was no accident that the New World was never discovered by way of the East, by way of the past. . . .

This rising of love to a higher estate, this relief and deliverance of a soul, stricken in its sensuous and selfish desires and unable to escape but by way of the infinite, is described very well in the following passage which occurs in the diary of an unhappy wife:

> Love's journey of liberation has many halting-places. Is it not written: "There are many dwelling-places in my Father's house"? After each stage the soul feels itself more completely stripped, more 'scoured'. In the course of my pilgrimage of suffering I have lost that unbridled craving for possession, the feeling of the 'my' that bulked so large in all my dearest loves. I never noticed that in grasping things I reduced them to my own measure. The less one grasps, the more one possesses. Love is an act of the will, not of the sensibility. The sensibility is rather the enemy of love; it thrusts it down into the domain of the instinct and keeps it there, allowing it to exult, moan and grow mad. . . . Then, after a brief and agonising paroxysm, comes death. Love is an act of continuous willing that makes for the unchangeable.[1] . . .

But to attain this condition of unchanging repose there is need to have faith: faith in the dawn night

[1] These notes are an expression of personal experience, not of absolute truths. Sensibility itself is the servant and ally of love; it becomes its enemy only as it abandons its subordinate rôle: a too exacting ally *ipso facto* becomes an enemy.

carries in its womb. The faded flowers of first love have still to be watered. It is a thankless task, for the petals have to be shed to make ready for the fruit. Man's unhappiness lies in his attachment to the flower, to the early rapture; seeing nothing beyond, he passes from flower to flower only to end by dying of hunger on a heap of dried petals. Such is the pitiful draining away of love. But he who survives the withering of these immediate joys is rewarded with a love that not only exhilarates but feeds. The flower has only its fragrance, but the fruit is fragrance and nourishment as well. . . . Love is no longer a thing of fleeting emotions, of ephemeral gifts; it is the silent interchange of substance, communion of soul with soul; not only has it nothing to fear from daily routine, but it is actually deepened and developed by habitual use. The intimacy of a life lived together, such a pitiless disperser of the shadow-love, gives true love strength, almost a kind of virginity:

> Apart from daily use, the gentle homely drabness
> of the unwearying hours,
> May one find sustenance, drink undefiled?
> Joy, too proud and solitary to sleep within the arms
> of habit, is but the ghost of joy. . . . Lacking life,
> it fears both sleep and habit:
> Usurping life, it fears lest rest's relaxing, less
> yielding to the threaded days, unmask the fraud.
> Awake, alert, but always transient, different—such
> must be the sham; illusion has no right to take its
> rest.

The trickling stream of habit washes off the paint,
The lie is shown for what it is in rest . . .
But thou, unchanging stream,
That flowest calmly between habit's banks,
Constant till all's forgotten, limpid as the void,
Eternity's pure child,
To thee the hours are sisters!—
Other draughts have made me drunk,
For me thy cup alone has poured out life . . .

Love, then, before it is purified, famishes man, because it lives on desire; but purified, love nourishes, because it lives on giving.

The "nights" of human love have the effect of restoring sex to its true place, of integrating the impulse of instinct in spiritual love. They realise a fundamental and complete unity between two persons, a unity required by their original love and already sensed by it in advance. For it is a mistake to suppose the awakening of love is merely a trick of the instinct. Those who try to reduce the lover's ideal to the simple play of animal needs contradict themselves by the very expressions they use. What is the meaning of such terms as "ruses of the instinct", "disguised sexuality" and so forth, which keep on recurring in everything they write? Why a ruse if there is no one to deceive? And why a disguise if there is no one to evade? If love were solely actuated by instinct there would be no need for these subterfuges: the very necessity to deceive implies the existence of a love above instinct. Not only so, but if instinct must needs assume the mask of "noble" values, if it must puff itself up to be justified by the spirit, it is because it knows its destiny is to be exalted by the spirit. The mask is the first stage, as it were, in the transfiguration; it serves as a priming. The cosmic impulse has to go on deceiving till it is finally mastered and transfigured by the *person*. The result of this mysterious antinomy is a higher unity, the supreme expression of the mysterious order of creation. Of all the human instincts, sex is farthest removed from conscience and spirit; none other is so deeply rooted in the impersonal and anonymous. Yet no other animal passion has so close an affinity with the things of the soul: none other raises such subtle and suppliant feelers to the summits to which man is capable of attaining. The other instincts—those, like hunger, which tend to the preservation of the individual—present themselves to consciousness as purely biological. They are very faintly "idealisable", and that is why they never wear masks! Sexuality, by aping the ideal, gives proof of its fundamental relationship to the ideal. It wears a mask, as an inward compromise and excuse, as long as it continues to seek its true image—sometimes, it must be admitted, with an alarming lack of success!

From the very first contact, then, between lovers, the thing that desire obscurely strives after is the spiritual reality of man, the unique and eternal soul. Unfortunately, however, sexuality has also other kinds of kinship with the spirit. If the sexual instinct adapts itself to spiritual love through the depth and subtlety of its pervading of human nature, it is perhaps even more closely allied, through its qualities of violence and gross sensuality, to the rebelliousness of the spirit and its unbridled will to power. Animal egotism answers to the egotism of the spirit. In each there is precisely the same ignoring of the object, the same incapacity to give. Instinct, as such, seeks no more in the partner than its own satisfaction: the will to power sees the human person merely as servile matter to conquer and rule. Moreover, in the human soul, as we have shown above, there is a close and deep relationship between sexuality and pride: the two things aggravate and devour one another. Many examples could be given. One of the most convincing is the humiliation and despair of the sexually impotent. . . .

Suffering and dryness, by momentarily interrupting the animal pleasures of the flesh and the spiritual delight in self-assertion, lead lovers, not to a sexless union, but one in which the love of *persons* makes a fresh discovery of the attraction of sex. This sexuality is a kind of product of the soul. Balance is achieved, and the human synthesis of sexual love. The vague feeling, that instinct has, of its own immortal nature is based on the feeling of the immortality of the person, and this is the very essence of love. It is only then, incidentally, that *human* sexuality displays its true treasures. In every soul there are spiritual depths and subtleties that are conditioned by the difference of sex but crushed and blighted by a carnal overcharging of it. The materialising of sexual attraction has been very costly to sexual love.[1] The attraction of sex is something very different from the love of a spiritual being endowed with sex. Rakes and debauchees are least capable of appreciating the secret depths of the feminine soul: Don Juan made a far poorer use of his sexual instinct than do many men who live perfectly chaste. . . . Whatever the apostles of the primacy of pleasure may say, a man cannot be fully sexual without first being fully personal, without being a man. Sexuality isolated from the person comes to nothing.

It is in this way love attains its full and perfect stature. Lovers, as Nietzsche observed, are not in love with their own inclination to love; what they love *first* is the being to whom they incline. They love the joy that comes to them through the being they love, but the being they love is not incidental to their joy: "I do not love you for what you give, I love you for what you are." The idol of the first love is dead. Creatures love one another, not as they are dreamed, but as God made them. Such love excludes neither pleasure nor suffering, far from it; but it lies in a region beyond both. It is like the life that animates two intermingling substances that nourish one another by merely existing:

> Evening sacrifice. Hitherto I have given you but
> happiness and suffering. Today I give my soul,
> This naked essence, drop of eternity, that cannot
> breathe out life with kisses, or flow away with tears.

[1] To make our meaning perfectly clear: we are not advocating a kind of Wagnerian angelism in matters of sex. The sexuality we are defending is a *human* sexuality, a thing of body and soul like man, but with a soul informing and ruling the body.

First, in you, I loved what you possessed. After
  that, your poverty I cherished. What I love today
  is *you*.
My love for you is simple: unguided, untranscended!
There follow after, joy and tears: delights and pains
  are mingled in its wake. But nothing goes before.
  No star gleams out above!

This masterful freedom in regard to things of sense
and time, the freedom that belongs of right to a
great love by which, in Dante's words, "man makes
himself eternal", is well described, I think, in the
following lines:

Only your silence now feeds my desire,
The tears I weep all other tears destroy.—
Give me your love, than any pain more dire,
Give me your love, more pure than any joy.

*   *   *

One last question, one we would merely touch on.
This ascent of human love we have been describing
—can it exist in the purely natural order, as something that can be the sole affection between creatures?
We think not. To be able to love a finite being in
spite of its worthlessness, because of its worthlessness,
to love it without bounds, one could only love as a
messenger of some surpassing reality. It is impossible
to have an absolute love for the negative as such.
But in a great love, even when it has not undergone
purification, a man is irrigated (as it were) by the
creature, as by a channel or vessel. The chosen soul,
at the dawning of love, is a messenger of the cosmic
plenitude; in love that has been purified, it is a

messenger of the divine plenitude. It first leads man into communion with the sensuous soul of the world to reveal to him later, by way of the Cross, the spiritual soul that creates and sustains the world. Its very emptiness is then loved as a gateway to Being. It is impossible to proceed far in the trans-figuring of human love unless—however veiled and implicit the manner—there is a love for God in the creature, and unless God, by way of the creature, gives himself. The heroic ascent of human love is possible only to those with a deep religious sense; it implies *at least* a vague awareness of the super-natural, a dim expectation of that abyss of divine love which calls eternally to all those lovers who have reached the farthest headlands of human love. Ultimately the essence of a great love between man and woman lies in the train of divine revelations and graces received into the soul through the chosen channel of another. Such self-effacement in favour of a secondary cause bears the stamp of what is deepest and subtlest in God's ways. The creature here gives more than itself—as the poet declares to his beloved: "Thy hands are richer than thy soul . . ." —it gives to another, chosen out from all the rest, the divine secret of the world and the human secret of the divine:

You have slain my dream . . .
And mingling with my soul you taught me that the
    world is one,
That in the eyes of love there is one name for all,
And that name a prayer!

For thee, I went down into the seamless depths, where
nothing separates or grades, where the whole
universe has neither high nor low, where but one
only creature sighs in presence of one only God . . .
Strait soul, of depths unfathomable . . . perfect in thy
poverty, weakness chosen out of boundless strength,
trembling supporter of the world and God!

PART TWO

INTRODUCTION

Of all human values, love is the one that promises most and performs least. None has such a portentous air of inevitability: none is so liable to deteriorate and turn false. As they kiss for the first time, even the most commonplace lovers murmur, "Always!" It is not enough that their hearts should be overflowing: their plenitude must be immortal. If they knew it would one day die, their fleeting happiness would be poisoned. Dante's great question—*How may man make himself eternal?*—weighs more heavily on the fervour of love than on any other impulse that inhabits the human soul.

It is to this question that the following thoughts aim to give some rudiments of an answer. It is a Christian answer. It is in the necessity for a religious fulfilment and a religious purification, in the effort to join human love to an absolute love, that the meaning of my conflicting statements must be sought. Love is something to be cursed or blessed, as it approaches the extremes of the idolatrous or the divine. When Goethe wrote, "The eternal feminine draws us ever upwards", it was not to contradict that hard wisdom of Ecclesiastes, who declares woman to be something even "bitterer than death". Is woman a gateway to God or an idol concealing him? It is because we believe in love's truth that we are severe upon its travesties. The heights correspond to the depths: it is only from what is high that it is possible to fall. Hell, perhaps, is only a paradise *closed*.

The one great problem is how to *open* the humble paradise of love, to turn the wall into a gate; and to this end, to create a common bond between lovers sufficiently strong to ensure its immortality. "To love", as Saint-Exupéry wrote so well, "is not to look at one another but to look in the same direction." As Christians we should add: it is to look and walk together beside God.

CHAPTER I

Body and Soul

THE PARADOX OF LOVE.—The root of all the discords and disasters, all the meannesses and follies that love brings in its train, lies in this: the love of the sexes is at once the commonest of all things and the rarest, the easiest and most difficult: alongside gross animal attraction, it carries in itself the need for the most personal, selective and solitary communion; it must include and unite both human extremes, the material and the divine. A woman happens to pass: instinct cries after her; in hot haste it persuades the soul that here is the chosen, the one and only. . . . Such is the birth of all love's illusions. Lips are kissed, the body is embraced, and eternity called on to justify all the imperfection of the present. Think you the soul will follow? Pull hard on the leash and the soul is strangled!

*　　*　　*

Love in its true form is something so mighty and profound, it implies such a harmonising of contrasts, that in this world it invites, it almost demands, a caricature. If we are not wholly raised up by sexual love, we are thrust down by it.

*　　*　　*

An unavoidable alternative faces human sexuality: either to be controlled and *exalted* by spiritual love, or else to be *prostituted* by spiritual sin.

*   *   *

The sign that distinguishes a decadent sexuality is its perpetually oscillating between platonic love and lust, between the dream and the mud.

*   *   *

THE TWO SOURCES OF JOY.—True joy is not that which flows down from the lips to the heart, it is that which surges up from the heart to the lips.

*   *   *

An eighteenth-century epigram, affixed to a portrait of Love, concludes with the line:

And so of dalliance I die.

This piece of triviality looks profound today. In the present age it is the feeble and foolish fashion to cry up pleasure: not pleasure in itself, but the chafed and impoverished caricature of sexual delight to which the moderns offer incense under the title of pleasure. So it is a relief to observe that in Voltaire's time men were still aware there are pleasures that kill. Indeed, among all human things, pleasure is the hardest to purify, to "deliver". It may always be objected that a love which can be dissipated by pleasure and "possession" is nothing more than the expectation of that pleasure: it is a mere physical tension and therefore deserves to die. But what does anyone know of it? And what, broadly speaking, does anyone know of the physiological states that condition and foster even the loftiest soaring of the human spirit? Who can tell the precise weight of spiritual purity, anguish or love, that the hard-strained cord of the flesh can *support*? And if the cord gives way, woe to the spiritual treasures that hang upon it! Pleasure can kill more than our expectation of pleasure. The pleasure that kills strikes at something beyond itself: it strikes *upwards*.

* * *

SEXUALITY, PAGAN AND CHRISTIAN.—Pagan love for woman, from Catullus to Pierre Louÿs, sees the soul through the body. Christian love regards the body, and loves it, by way of the soul. The first diminishes the soul to the measure of the frail and perishable flesh: hence all its complaints about the deceptive brevity of love and happiness. The second gives to the flesh all the amplitude and permanence of the soul—the dogma of the resurrection of the body. Who, then, has the greater reverence for the flesh? He who prostitutes everything to it, including the spirit? Or he who weds it with the eternal purity of the spirit?

* * *

Love, the dilating of the flesh: egotism, the contracting of the flesh—an oscillation between two poles, each as terrestrial as the other. Perhaps man will begin to be saved when he realises, with his whole soul, that what he calls his love is just as vain, just as subject to carnal necessity, as what he calls his egotism. The only love that truly takes us out of ourselves is that which proceeds not from nature but from grace.

*   *   *

Violence and Depth.—Often the violence of a passion suggests depth, whereas it usually excludes it. A violently agitated surface catches the eye and stirs the emotions more readily than a silent abyss. That is why passions aroused by the flesh and the imagination—particularly sexual love and political infatuations—are all so intoxicating and deceptive. They are as intoxicating as the spectacle of a storm at sea, and as fugitive. . . .

*   *   *

The drama of a double degrading of love. Spiritually man ranks higher than woman, carnally he ranks lower. In order to love a woman he must descend spiritually. But he cannot stay at woman's level, in the intermediate zone of "heart": he must sink into the flesh—and drag woman after him.

*   *   *

What I sought in you was a soul. All I found was a heart. . . .

*   *   *

A materialistically minded scientist would seek the soul with his scalpel. He is not likely to succeed—any more than lovers, seeking love in pleasure, are ever likely to find it with kissing.

*   *   *

The conflict between "flesh and spirit" takes place chiefly in the flesh. That in us which scorns the flesh and holds the joys of the senses to be degraded and vile, is neither truly spirit nor truly ideal; it is the imagination and its figments, the "refined" and "mystical" element in the flesh. . . . There is nothing impure about pleasure except in the eyes of the dreamer, for here the two adversaries are on precisely the same ground, and one decreases while the other grows.

The age when conflict between body and spirit is most acute, when disgust at things of the flesh is most violent, is just the dreaming age, when imagination is in highest ferment: adolescence.

*   *   *

THE PROBLEM OF FIDELITY.—There are two opposite poles in the fidelity of man and woman in love: the one is animal, the other spiritual. There is a merely physical fidelity, well expressed by the common phrase: to have "under one's skin". When passions take a hold on the depths of sensibility they acquire the constancy and necessity of an organic need. The faithfulness of many lovers is very similar to that of a dog to its master. What is inconstant in us is not animal; it is a spiritual thing enslaved to animality, or in other words it is the sin of curiosity, infiltrated into the flesh it infatuates. High above all is that other fidelity, the fidelity of the mature spirit that wholly controls the senses. To pass from inconstancy to fidelity is not to go from flesh to spirit, but from the *carnal* spirit to the spirit *incarnate*.

*   *   *

LOVE AND MARRIAGE.—Outside marriage, or what tends towards marriage—and by marriage I mean the unity of two destinies, something living and indissoluble, not society's official permit to love!— the union of man and woman must be illusion or squalor. It is very often both; a mixture of ether and mud. For in every sphere it is the easiest thing in the world to pass from chimera to dirt. The breaking cloud resolves itself into mud.

CHAPTER II

Women

FOR a woman in love, man is an end. But for a man, however much he is in love, woman is always a means: no doubt the highest means—a mixture of means and end—but never purely an end. *Woman was created for man, and man for God.*[1]

*　　*　　*

Man desires, woman gives. Woman need not be shocked at the selfishness of the male. Her own aspiration being merely to give herself, it is perfectly normal, and just as well for her, that man's aspiration should be simply to take her. What woman demands from man is not a love free from desire (*pace* the idealists, that is the last thing she worries about) it is *constancy in desiring her.* She is ready to be a mere prey. But in this she demands the impossible, for the essence of desire is the changing of its objective. One prey devoured, it is necessary to hunt others.

*　　*　　*

[1] This is from St Paul. Thinking it sufficiently well known I omitted to say so in the first edition of this book. I mention it now owing to the many reproaches I have received from Catholic readers who attributed the authorship of the remark to me. They described it as inhuman—and even heretical!

KNOWLEDGE AND LOVE.—Women think of the object of their love in the second person, they must always call him "you"; that is why they never search for truth. Only men can dedicate themselves to something that is never addressed but always referred to as "it". Women feel the need to speak *to* someone, men to speak *of* something.

* * *

There is no sure recipe for making a woman happy. It is just a matter of fate. A woman is happy when she is in love, and it doesn't matter whom she loves or how her lover behaves. Deep down in the soul there must be a mutual and entirely involuntary adaptation. Otherwise nothing is of any avail: a sense of duty, the best intentions in the world, are about as much use as a performing bear. The utmost they can do, in the most favourable circumstances, is to give the pale illusion of a love that has never been born, or prolong the agony of a love that is already dying. Happiness, here, is not created by kindliness. It is all in vain that I *wish* your good, unless deep within you I already *am* your good. . . .

* * *

If we ask women for understanding there are few who will not deceive us; if we ask them for devotion there are few who will not surprise us.

* * *

A man in love feels bound to justify his love logically; morally, too, since morals follow from logic; and in the eyes of public opinion, which follows from morals! (A man has always an eye on public opinion, even when he despises it: for then he is not indifferent, he is merely cynical. . . .) A woman, on the other hand, is content simply to love: her love is *justificatus in semetipsum.* When she gives herself—even in unlawful or ridiculous circumstances—she looks no farther; she has a feeling of well-being, or the "good conscience" of a creature that fulfils its purpose, realises its destiny. For her, the offering of herself is the last reality: the thing that justifies and explains all, not needing to be justified or explained by anything else. Whereas a man in love is never entirely satisfied with himself; he always expects his reason to find some excuse or alibi for his passion. . . .

*   *   *

A woman's love is naturally less selfish and inconstant than a man's; generally speaking, it requires no effort for a woman to be devoted and faithful to the man she loves. But that does not make her affection altogether innocent of self-seeking. She desires the happiness of the loved one, but the happiness must come from none but herself: "I want you to be happy, but only through me!" Moreover the purifying of a woman's love means ridding herself, not of selfishness precisely, but of a kind of greedy and exclusive altruism. To love truly, man has to overcome just ordinary selfishness, woman a sort of selfishness *à deux*.

*   *   *

The amoralism of women proceeds principally from the fact that they have no sense of the relative. They are wholly immersed in the love of the moment, they have no idea how to *portion out* their giving. Morals are primarily a matter of portioning out.

*   *   *

I had known him a long time. I thought I could read his soul like a book. And now a woman, who is the friend of both of us, has just revealed to me all the vivid tenderness of his character! It is one of the subtlest pleasures of social life, discovering what is deepest in a friend through the eyes of a woman. . . .

*   *   *

Women complicated? . . . Certainly not! They are strangely simple, transparent and easy to understand. Close your arms about a woman and you contain the whole of her; give her a kiss and it goes straight to her soul. It is we who complicate things where they are concerned, and we call it *their* complexity. The so-called complexity of women is simply man's inability to realise their simplicity.

*   *   *

FEMININE CANDOUR.—A woman who gives herself to a man "for nothing" imagines the mere fact of his acceptance implies, on his part, a profound bond of affection. Alas, the man who is so shallow, fickle and athirst for selfish pleasure, as to accept such a gift *immediately*, is naturally incapable of deep attachment or fidelity. Here the promptest to receive are the least inclined to give. Their readiness to accept all is a clear indication they will give nothing in return. . . .

* * *

Women will always respond, and be ready to give everything, as soon as an appeal is made to their *redemptive instinct*. This is a tendency that belongs to their very nature: it is as deep as their maternal instinct—and probably part and parcel of it. The lower type of man finds this an almost infallible method of seduction. The natural result is an added befoulment, a *double* sinking into the mire. But what is that to instinct?

* * *

DIALOGUE.—*He*: I will give myself perhaps, but you must first accept my God. *She*: I will accept your God perhaps, but you must first give yourself. . . .

* * *

To a woman in love.—Do not lose yourself completely in your lover. Keep something of your virginity even in the act of self-surrender: keep something back— something you deny, not to your lover, but to your lover's desire. If you allow him to absorb you entirely, if you abandon yourself wholly to his passion of today, what is left to sustain his frailty tomorrow? That in you which resists him in the hour of his joy may help to keep him afloat in the hour of his distress. But if you become absolutely one with him, how will you help him? A drowning man does not clutch at his own heart.

That is the mystery of emotional assimilation. The being we hold dearest, who allows herself to be completely mastered and absorbed, has no help to offer in our greatest trials and temptations. Does this mean that the very completeness of the gift is what renders it useless? We must distinguish here between interior aid and exterior aid. The soul that loses itself in another continues to dwell in it as a kind of *superfluous organ*; its intimate presence, deep within the other, has the effect of nourishing and furthering its life. But it is not enough to afford nourishment from within, when what is needed is salvation from without.

*   *   *

Idolatry.—He worships a woman. You think such idolatry deserves to be punished? No need to worry. His idol will see to that, in a way that will more than satisfy your indignation—or even your malice!

CHAPTER III

True Love

LOVE is pure when its thirst for happiness gives way to its passion for unity. As long as two beings are joined together by the mere desire for happiness, they are not truly in love, they are still parted. Love is the union of two lives, not two joys.

*   *   *

It is thus that true love tends to reduce the opposition between happiness and suffering. These two states of the soul, on the ordinary level so fiercely exclusive of one another, become on a higher plane two aspects of the same reality, a reality that contrives to absorb and control both. Love liberates and purifies both joy and pain: it purges the first of its sordid and fitful elements, the second of revolt and despair.

*   *   *

Love is no fleeting spark, struck from the clashing of two desires; it is an undying flame, blazing up from the fusion of two destinies.

*   *   *

The worth of a love is that of the lover. This is true in a sense. But love, the fire that is kindled by

the contact of two souls, is not to be identified with
either of them separately, nor even with the sum of
them both. It is a new and entirely unforeseen
reality. In a successful love there is much more than
the sum of two beings in love; in an unsuccessful love
there is much less.

*   *   *

Magnus amor.—Rapture and security combined.
A rapture without an awakening, without a bitter
dawn to follow: a flame that feeds on itself and leaves
no ashes.

*   *   *

So natural, that what we love we prize,
We would have all men see it through our eyes.
                                        (*Corneille*)

To be unable to love what is not esteemed is a
sign of health in love, for here health is unity, harmony between mind and passion. At the opposite
extreme lies passion in anarchy, a stranger to the
soul it enslaves. "What does that man know of
love who has never been constrained to despise
what he loves?" (Nietzsche).

*   *   *

Eadem velle . . .—Only a common love of the same
things can prove a mutual love: I call this central
law of love *the principle of the included third.* There can
be a selfishness shared by two; a selfishness shared by
three is more difficult to conceive. This third thing
that proves love may be a creature, or God, or a

work of man, or a mission in life—any of these may be shared, or several, but at least one must be there. The *solus ad solam* is not a healthy state of affairs: even in the highest form of it, mystical love, it is the love of one's neighbour that proves love for God. Without this third reality in common, love can be no more than a mingling of selfishness and illusion—in short, an idolatry. A true union between two beings is not so much a giving of the self to another; it is rather two giving themselves to the same something else. And that, of course, is the meaning of the old dictum: *eadem velle, eadem nolle.*

Besides, how can one conceive of the birth of a true affection between two beings who do not feel, from the very start, that they are linked by a common inclination to the same things? In the absence of a community of interest, love is but a vulgar token of conquest and monopoly. It is a common experience that affections are painfully fragile that boast of self-sufficiency (nothing but us!) and do not rest on the giving of the self to something in common. Mutual love quickly perishes of inanition unless it has a common love to support it.

*   *   *

HAPPINESS AND THE ABSOLUTE.—As far as happiness is concerned, the absolute is incapable of being realised in this world. But for their failures in the pursuit of happiness men have a way of taking their revenge on love.

*   *   *

Love has failed you? Take a look at yourself. Were you not always confusing love with happiness? It is not love that has failed you: you have never loved.

*   *   *

Nolite quaerere.—Happiness is perhaps the only thing to which the injunction "seek and you shall find" does not apply. The pursuit of happiness sets up a tension in the soul that makes happiness impossible.

*   *   *

Walk in your love, but never expect joy to keep up with you step by step. Happiness is not *love's shadow*. While love goes forward, happiness may often seem to loiter—or even to be going back. But when your love attains its goal, which is God, joy will swoop to its side and never leave it any more.

*   *   *

There can be such a mingling of two souls that they need one another to exist, let alone to grow.

*   *   *

THE ABSOLUTE.—We have only to love someone absolutely and we have no further need to ask of him—the absolute.

*   *   *

DETACHMENT AND FULFILMENT.—I love you, and you cannot be mine. But if I love you enough, if I drink the water near enough to its source, there need be no defilement in my love. To ask all is the same as to ask nothing. It is only the partial gifts that are forbidden.

* * *

There is a love that saves and a love that corrupts —and that depends less on the giver than the receiver. Nothing so spoils and corrupts any being, who is already disposed to be selfish and soft, as a general atmosphere of affection and "understanding". Only one who hates himself can safely be loved. Christianity, by uniting love to the Cross, has purged it of its poison.

* * *

MODESTY AND DISSIMULATION.—There is a strong resemblance between their outward manifestations; but how different their inner origin! Modesty is born of a fear of falsehood; dissimulation of a fear of truth. Modesty veils itself from the superficial glance, the leering scrutiny, the false light. Dissimulation veils itself from the true light. Modesty fears the misunderstanding of its secret, dissimulation fears its own may be all too clearly seen. One is afraid of being judged by appearances, the other trembles to be judged by truth. Hugo sums it all up in a single line:

Innocence goes veiled, wrongdoing hides.

* * *

LOVE AND FRAILTY.—Frailty lies when it speaks of love. He who has nothing to give to himself will get nothing from anyone else. Man can only give and receive as he is capable of suffering. His capacity for communion depends on his capacity for solitude.

*   *   *

Every lover is frail. But is it love that makes him frail—or frailty that makes him love?

*   *   *

THE PERFECTION OF HUMAN LOVE.—To taste the worthlessness of the beloved, but without bitterness, without disillusionment or revolt. The nothingness in you is what calls for worship: it is all that may. . . .

*   *   *

THE MYSTERY OF LOVE.—The encounter of two poverties makes riches. One nothingness has only to surrender itself to another to create a god.

*   *   *

I judge of the purity and soundness of an attachment by the feeling of freedom it leaves me.

*   *   *

No need to worry about what is held most precious. There is nothing less importunate to a man than his ultimate destiny. With a great love he can take plenty of liberties: he feels it is impossible to lose it and is not afraid of being parted from it. Those for whom our love is complete are no more burdensome to us or tyrannical than our own soul: we freely leave

them, to find them again later—just as, after the
eclipse of sleep, we find ourselves again when we wake.

The passion that is an exclusive possession can
never be deep: it is not woven into the inner pattern
of our destiny; the more it feels itself threatened the
tighter it clings. The grip of a drowning man is
something there is no shaking off.

*   *   *

A true love of creatures is essentially religious. "I
love you as God wishes you to be." On the other
hand, the false love of creatures is something sacrilegious: "I refuse to accept you as you were originally
created."

*   *   *

A bad love—I almost wrote a "literary" love—is
recognisable by the fact that it plays at being divine.
(God is the being who loves only himself and his
creation: for him, nothing anterior has any existence!)
Such a love regards the beloved as a work of art
to be realised: "loving" is then like constructing
a novel! There is always the desire to "draw out"
the loved one from the lover's imagination. Such a
"creative" process is poles apart from true love,
which is consent and surrender, an attitude of holy
passivity towards a being not made by us, but
given us from without. The artist creates, whereas the
lover (as it were) allows himself to be created. The
former endows the object, that he draws out of
himself and projects, with the form dictated by his

desire and his dreaming; the latter is content to let his desire and his dreaming take the form of a reality exterior to himself, anterior to himself and received into himself. In the one case the subject informs the object, in the other it is informed by it. . . .

This morbid encroachment of the artistic activity upon the things of the heart leads finally to the poisoning and death of love. It is to clash with the impossible to expect artistic *projection* to take the place of loving *acceptance*. And it is not without humour that so many people, after generously drugging their affections with narcissism, complain bitterly that love is an artifice and a romantic fiction—the very things they had always confused it with!

*   *   *

LOVE AND NECESSITY.—I never chose you. I should have loved you ill if I had had to choose you. No one chooses God: he stands alone. It is the same with certain of God's gifts; they impose themselves with the same force of necessity as God himself; like him they exclude all weighing and choosing. You are not the *elect* (*prima inter pares*), you are unique.

Even the chances that brought about our meeting were part of me. In the life of every man there are decisive moments when chance is completely the slave of necessity. At such times it is absurd to talk about chance, to use the hypothetical "if". From the moment you came into existence you had no alternative but to come to me. Souls are not created by halves. There is no separating your love from the events that gave birth to it: your entry into my life was essentially part of you.

> My heart told me: each soul is sister to another
> . . . their fate is, soon or late, to meet.
>
> (*Lamartine*)

*   *   *

An idiotic and dangerous myth, this of a sister soul created specially for each one of us, only needing to be met with to realise an earthly paradise of love. Of course, to the ripening of a great love, a minimum of pre-established harmony is indispensable; but in the case of hundreds of women this minimum of agreement is realised *a priori* in the first man they meet; in the case of hundreds of men, in the first woman they meet. To ignore this truth calls for all the innocence and candour of youth. And plenty of pride too: a man must believe himself unique and solitary as a god, a god that only another divine personage, as solitary and unique as he, can love and understand.

A solitary Tristan for a solitary Yseult: the deifying of human love, like all other idolatries, leads straight to the destruction of the idol itself. Don Juan is none other than Tristan's son, and he bears a painful resemblance to his father. Both are victims of the myth of the *unique, perfect and predestined mistress:* one thinks he possesses her, the other is still searching. Both are believers in the absolute, in the paradise of love; but it is a paradise to be had for nothing, to be entered on the ground floor, created merely by the encounter and the presence.

Actually, at the hour of first meeting, the unique and irreplaceable harmony between two souls is no more than a vague outline on the stony matrix of illusion. It is from daily association, with its shared joys, sorrows, efforts and sacrifices, that it achieves its firm and unalterable form. The "sister soul", the "other half", is not something given *a priori*, but *a posteriori*: it requires our love and loyalty to create it. It might have been another; but after the trial of love it could only be this one. The bride who is unique has to earn her title: true monogamy, the ultimate fusion of two destinies, is to be found at the end of love, not at the beginning.

*   *   *

There is no contradiction between the last two aphorisms. They are true at two different levels. Eternal necessity is apparent even in the things that depend on time and chance. But it is something that can be recognised and accepted only by the pure in heart. It is a serious illusion—and an open door to all kinds of disappointments—to clothe earthly events prematurely in the absolute. First love is not necessarily eternal love.

*   *   *

Great passions, temptations, etc.—In certain extreme cases the mere fact of envisaging the possibility of something is enough to render it inevitable.

*   *   *

What I chiefly desire to receive from you is what I have already! All that is sacred in me I shall possess unshadowed only when I receive it at your hands and lips. You give me nothing unless you give me myself. Before I can have rest in my soul I must receive it from you as alms.

*   *   *

The love of a creature can create nothing in us. But it can *liberate* everything. Without another's intervention, without external warmth, our greatest strength remains for ever impotent, for ever in chains. Who has ever touched his own depths without the help of another, without being able to say to friend or lover: You gave me to myself, I received my soul at your hands?

*   *   *

LOVE AND SILENCE.—Our words may differ: it is enough that our silences agree. There is no true union between two beings unless understanding precedes and measures utterance. Possessing the same ideas, the same desires and ambitions, avails nothing to the expression of them without the possibility of communing in the same silence. . . . The words uttered have value only as they issue from this silence; words heard mean nothing unless they leave mute traces in the soul and add something to the treasure of silence already there.

It is not from what is said that love is born, it is from what is left unsaid. People meet and part as lovers when no more has been said than a few trite platitudes—interspersed with long silences! The word gives birth to friendship, silence to love. . . . Speaking is just as embarrassing to new lovers as silence to a pair of new friends.

*　　　*　　　*

MAGNUS AMOR.—It rises like a river, from an inner plenitude, an upsurging from below. Like a river it grows stronger and wider as it flows: every accident it encounters becomes its tributary, so does every joy, still more every tear. And as a river finally loses itself in the sea, so love, at death, becomes immortalised in God.

*　　　*　　　*

DESIRE AND POSSESSION.—The things that are truly God's gifts always exceed our expectations. We never, in practice, receive what we expect: always less or more. In what matters most, we receive desire with the object, thirst with the draught. The self-giving of the beloved *creates* a place in the heart to be filled. Awareness of the abyss that each contains comes only when it is filled. . . .

*　　　*　　　*

LOVE AND RESEMBLANCE.—Here are two women I admire and respect. I cannot love either of them: one is too like me, the other is not like me at all. It is impossible to love either one's double or one's opposite. What love demands is a discreet admixture of identity and difference.

*　　　*　　　*

Whom would anyone find most intolerable? His double, if such a one could exist, his living copy: a being who would be another, a stranger, but with no novelty to conceal, no mystery! We should hate our double to the precise extent to which we love our ego. The *alter ego* is another matter: identity of love depends on difference of nature.

* * *

LOVE'S CRISES.—Some are unfaithful because their love changes its object, others because their power to love grows enfeebled. These latter are the nobler types. But they do not get to the depths of their love. Great love is allied to an eternal principle, one exempt from all hazards, transcending our subjective power to love and surviving it if it perishes. That is the reason why a man can say, in spite of all the potential deaths that dwell in him: I will love you always.

* * *

DEATH AND LOVE.—The great privilege of the dead is their unchangeableness. They no longer have the melancholy capacity to alter or to retract the message they have once delivered to us. Because they are unable to betray us, we can confidently rely on them. For this reason every great love is akin to death: it has the same quality of finality, it offers the same guarantees of unchangeable loyalty. Those who truly love are in a sense already dead: like the dead they are exempt from change and falsehood. Their dwelling is already *the heaven of the fixed stars*.

They no longer inhabit this imperfect world where generation is for ever being answered by corruption. This would explain the affinity between love and death, of which all true lovers have a sure presentiment. . . .

*   *   *

True faithfulness consists in the continual rebirth of what has been born already. Such are the poor seeds of eternity sown by God in time: unfaithfulness rejects them, false fidelity mummifies them. Only birth has any charm, say the lovers of change; but what cannot be reborn has never been born. (In this world there are more miscarriages than births.) The act of picking the flower is no less pure than that of sowing the seed—and he who cannot await the harvest has never known the joy and the love of the sower: he has simply opened his hands and gone through the motions of sowing in a trance; he has not sown. . . .

*   *   *

ANTIPATHY.—There are some people who are fated to irritate us—unintentionally, perhaps by mistake. But it is only an apparent mistake. If we are wrong about their *manners* we are not wrong about their *nature*: it is a true intuition of a deep disharmony that causes us to misinterpret whatever they do. When someone is repugnant for what he is, there is nothing he can do—even with the best intentions in the world—that can please us.

*   *   *

In you I have a refuge where nothing can deceive me; where, even if you would, you could never kill my love. I am so wedded to your soul at its depths that I entirely escape your powers of destruction. I live too close to you for your blows to touch me. . . .

CHAPTER IV

False Love

ORIGINAL SIN.—Original sin has affected love in quality rather than in quantity. It has not so much diminished as debased and corrupted it; it has vulgarised rather than enfeebled it. This is intolerable: any but the coarsest and shallowest natures would far rather be hated than loved after such a fashion. A vulgar love is a *winded* love. It is a love that stops short at the material, whether in things or persons: it refuses to go on into the centre and spirit of beings, it refuses to go on to God. Here vulgarity becomes one with idolatry.

* * *

In idolatrous love there is one thing, and only one, that is never lacking: one thing, at least, that can be always counted upon. And that is deception. There is at any rate this much truth in it—and that is falsehood!

* * *

Woman promises what only God can perform. There is no occasion to upbraid her for it. Surely it is marvellous enough that there should be such a

promise. Woman is simply the enticement God uses.
There is none so irresistible.

*   *   *

Woman's is the closest presence. That is the secret
of her attraction: it is easier to fall into a woman's
arms than to mount up to God. But this presence,
close as it is, is never interior. And that is how she
disappoints us. God, on the other hand, is the
remotest of all beings. No warm embrace, no glow of
passion here. Yet his presence can penetrate to the
depth of our being and fill that void in the soul
which the sublimest love of woman leaves empty.

*   *   *

When the only purpose love serves is to leave us
alone after the illusion of deliverance, to make our
loneliness a thousandfold more bitter, more hopeless,
more worthy of the terrible pity of God—then it will
not have been in vain.

*   *   *

Loneliness is bitter. But it is something bitterer
still for two to be lonely together and so make one
loneliness. Communion spoilt is the worst of all
solitudes.

*   *   *

The love of woman is the trial of our solitude. He
who has never hoped everything of a woman has not

learnt how incurable his solitude is—incurable, and therefore divine. Purification at the centre: after really confusing God with woman it is no longer possible to confuse anything with God. The floor has been swept clean!

*　　　*　　　*

For most women, to wish a man's good is an almost certain means of not doing him any good. The good they wish us prevents their seeing the good we need.

*　　　*　　　*

HATRED AND LOVE.—Consider the history of everything, the history of men and peoples and ideas: everywhere you see conflict preceding unity, for the sake of unity. Would not love, then, be hatred come to maturity, turned to gold in the nick of time? Or rather, would not hatred seem to be a shift, a useful detour, a roundabout way to love?

*　　　*　　　*

A woman would help you? Take care. She will sit on your burden. . . .

*　　　*　　　*

Which is the more pessimistic as regards women? Not he who complains idiotically that they are wholly evil and their love a lie. Rather he who believes in their love but thinks it useless; who thinks they are good, but to no purpose; that they do us harm while wishing us well. It is infinitely less bitter to believe in the absence of love than in a love doomed to frustration—in a man-killing bear than in a performing bear. There is no worse tyrant than a well-meaning tyrant.

* * *

To a woman.—You may be big enough to understand me, but are you big enough to *support* me?

* * *

Foretaste of hell.—To live with a person one cannot endure—and cannot do without.

* * *

The limitations of love.—Your love can remove mountains? Probably. But what about the imponderables! Everything would be too easy if it were simply a matter of levelling mountains, if great passions had only great obstacles to contend with. But you are surrounded by malign necessities that are too insignificant for your love to deal with; yet they continue to wreak havoc on it. You brandish the heroic sword with which you have rid yourself of giants; but there is an infuriating gnat that keeps humming round your head. What good is a sword against that?

* * *

The tragedy of love.—It does not consist in the union (as they think) of two people in love who have nothing to give each other. There is nothing tragic

13

in that, it's just a common blunder. It is when two
people, who can give one another everything,
actually give nothing, and that through a mere
lack of external adaptation, doing a little too much or
not quite enough.

                    *   *   *

THE PROBLEM OF "INCONSTANCY".—Is it inconstancy that makes us forget some people, or is it
lack of adaptation, a misunderstanding or a "mis-
deal"? As long as my relations with superficial
people have remained superficial I have managed to
avoid disillusionment and disloyalty. But whenever
I have expected more of anyone than he had it in
him to give, I have always been compelled to break
with him and forget. And this, not through inconstancy or any craving for change; but because, in
love, the obligation to withdraw is the same as the
necessity to die. How often one regrets having gone
too far, either with a friend or with a woman; of
having allowed one's love to overflow, beyond that
superficial level where some true exchange was
possible, on to another and deeper level where
disillusionment was inevitable! Alas, in cases like
that there is no going back. But it would have been
delightful to have stopped in time. Inconstancy, here,
is merely a way of retrieving a mistake, of remaining
faithful to oneself.

                    *   *   *

Granum veritatis.—The love of woman, proclaims
the cynic, brings us the shallowest joys and the

profoundest sorrows. The sight of happy lovers suggests the pitying thought: why should everyone in this world have to serve an apprenticeship for hell?

*　　*　　*

LOVE AND SLAVERY.—When you become someone's slave, you cease to be his servant and become his tyrant. . . .

*　　*　　*

Here are lovers lying to each other. Both know they are lying; but as long as love lasts, each of them believes in the sincerity of the other. Each expects the other to be absolutely truthful and pure. But such a demand, and such credulity on the part of love, are a sufficient proof that man was made for God. Any love may promise, but only God can perform.

*　　*　　*

I understand how "love", as it is described by Proust, implies necessarily irritation and hatred towards the beloved. It is a dreadful punishment, to be hopelessly isolated in one's own narcissism yet to be somehow compelled to run after other beings, pursuing a love that is utterly impossible. In such a case man is bound to hate his partner: he has nothing to give her, nothing to receive from her; all her presence does is to give cruel emphasis to his own lack of self-sufficiency, his own impotence to give himself.

*   *   *

DEATH AND LOVE.—I happened to read a couple of Victor Hugo's letters: one was addressed to his fiancée, the other led up to his breach with Sainte-Beuve. The first was merely an emphatic trifle, a glittering nothing—in short, a lie. But in the other —what precision, what pithy substance, what *truth*! What it amounts to is that in this world death is truer than love, that death is perhaps the only thing on earth that never lies—the purest image of God.

*   *   *

SEXUAL LOVE.—Ever since it has draped itself unwarrantably in the absolute and the ideal, the attraction of sex has become the basest and vulgarest form of love. Religion, "escape", has a place in this paltry business. Love is God. That is why men, who would never blush at eating or sleeping, nevertheless blush to be in love. It is an unconscious shame at worshipping a god so base. . . .

*   *   *

Your solitude weighs heavily on you? If it is the foolish bleating solitude of a stray sheep, it deserves to die in a woman's arms; but if it is the profound solitude of a shepherd's heart, a solitude that bears the stamp of the divine, guard yourself from love. Take a woman for your need, your pleasure, your torment, but look higher than that for your solitude's grave. . . .

Your solitude weighs heavily on you? Wait for God to ripen it, to become one with it. Or else procure an abortion, take it to the common slaughter-house, find a woman. But with your solitude slain in the egg you will have lost all chance of a higher communion. It is unified that you must climb to heaven, not coupled.

*　　*　　*

The thing that is essentially and hopelessly vulgar is not *expecting* everything of a woman —that is a trial often necessary even for the best. It is *finding* everything in a woman.

*　　*　　*

MARRIAGE.—The quality of a love can be judged from the conversation between a husband and wife after they have been married several years. As a rule it turns on mere scandal or worldly-interest: it is rarely above the level of the office or porter's lodge.

*　　*　　*

LOVE AND CHOICE.—Like to like. That is true enough for friendship, but what about love? When a man we know intimately introduces us to his friend, we never get a surprise: we know already the kind of friends he is likely to have. But if he presents us to the woman he loves, we can expect anything. To solve the mystery of certain unions one would have to apply to the demon whose task it is "to confound springs and thirstings". . . .

* * *

You say you love me? And you would have me make an effort to keep you? But as soon as a woman has to be "kept" she is not worth the keeping. Perish the love that does not begin by offering repose!

* * *

THE DOWNWARD CURVE.—You used to be *sacred* to me: you have become merely *dear*. The heart—that vulgar, wayward soul of the flesh—has banished the soul, the divine heart of the spirit. I love you. Yesterday that meant: I bless you. Today it means: I want you.

* * *

With most men, love rides upon desire; but the flanks of desire are none too sound. To travel far, you have to take care of your mount. It is far less important to eat than to be able to put up with hunger. Love has nothing, once it has all it desires. It is condemned, like the poor, to "live on privations"—or die.

* * *

"See with what shining eyes Virtue abhors me," says Rostand's Don Juan. With many people, and especially in matters of sex, the passion to judge is due to resentment—resentment at not having been a party to the sin.

* * *

Lebensneid.—Our worst enemy is he who guesses, senses our joy, yet knows not what it is. So it is with women, whose hearts and sensibilities are frozen, in the presence of a woman who is both loving and beloved. *Hatred of the unknown joy* is the most devouring and inextinguishable of all hates. The envious know it exists and at the same time they are aware it is not for them: there is no partaking of it, no dreaming even of its savour. Such is the scandal that calls forth every vengeance. It is for that the Pharisees killed God, and still slay all who bear any resemblance to him. . . .

* * *

Soft, crawling, parasite-like people: it is precisely these who think themselves indispensable. To the extent their feebleness has need of others, their vanity persuades them that others have need of them. Only the necessitous believe themselves necessary. If the ivy were conscious, it would be convinced it was performing a sacred duty to the oak. It is for your good I cling to you, it would declare *amorously*.

* * *

LOVE AND THE CHILD.—No need for any sequel to our love, murmur husband and wife in the secrecy of their souls: it must leave no traces, it must be as though it had never been. And actually it has no being! If a child were the result, it would gainsay that comfortable nothingness in our "union"; it would make it look as though we actually *had* loved, as though something *real* had passed between us. How intolerable, that anything so solid and true could come of the fleeting contact of flesh and dreaming! Why then! Will not tomorrow's wind blow all that away? Will our kisses become flesh and blood, will the mask that was our love give place to a face? It is perfectly normal, this attitude of a loveless couple that refuse a child: it is not merely that the possible child is an *encumbrance*, it is an *anomaly*. A love that is essentially nothing is logical in declining to have *being* as its result.

*   *   *

You grieve over its falsehoods. But if love were not true, and if you had not this truth within yourself, how could you bewail its falsehoods? Falsehood is a truth that has been run over and lies there writhing ridiculously in the mire. The falsehood of love is a wound in the heart of God—a wound turned septic. But the wound itself bears witness to the flesh.

*   *   *

A woman has lied to you; you have been deceived by someone who counterfeited piety. From these deceptions you draw arguments respectively against love and faith. But the deception itself is a tribute to true religion and pure love. Would you be so mortified in the depths of your soul by an incompetent cook or an indifferent barber? It hurts you to see something profaned. That shows it is sacred. The truest measure of the splendour of the form is your vexation at seeing the form caricatured.

CHAPTER V

Love's Torment

LOVE is not heavy. The branch breaks only when the bird flies away. I am not broken by your leaning upon me, only when you desert me.

* * *

Love is a centrifugal force: it should fly from the subject to the object. Consequently when a being to whom we have given our love proves empty or unworthy, nothing is more atrociously unnatural than to "withdraw" that love. Nothing is more fatally inhuman than to snatch back love from its object and to draw back into oneself what should naturally go forth. Love that flows out gives sustenance, that which is reabsorbed is poisonous.

* * *

The *catastrophic* element in a great passion: that intolerable mixture of strength and weakness—feeling all one's strength stolen, usurped, enslaved by a single weakness!

* * *

The sweetness of divine love: giving ourselves to one whom our love *cannot make suffer*. But this thorn of human love, this bitterness and pitiful leaning upon a being incapable of supporting itself, already wavering . . .!

*   *   *

I do not want to be loved. It was a long time before I understood the integrity of despair in this saying of Pascal's. It is not a cry of fatigue or selfishness, nor yet of a fearful, all-encompassing asceticism; it is the cry of one who has measured all too well his own capacity for disillusioning and torturing another; it is a final cry of pity. "For love of yourself, do not love me; do not put your lips to my empty, all too fragile cup. . . ." Ah, that dawning self-consciousness, when our love for our fellow-men is so great that we dare not ask to be loved by them!

*   *   *

Pascal wrote these words in pity: he would associate no one else in the pain and emptiness he bore within himself. It was a miracle of clear-sightedness and resignation, but a calumny on true love. For a lover, the worst of evils is the not sharing everything with the beloved—even, and especially, pain and emptiness. Pascal would have been willing to be loved if he had understood to what oblivion of happiness love can lead.

*   *   *

St John's answer to Pascal is: "He has seen his brother, and has no love for him; what love can he have for the God he has never seen?" The whole issue between Pascal and St John is whether the loves of this world have a negative or positive function: whether creatures are solely walls to mortify and frustrate us and so send us back to God, or whether they can be bridges—to lead us to God. The symbol of the bridge, it seems to me, is more Christian than the symbol of the wall. To reach the other bank we must set foot on the bridge: that is why I desire to be loved. But unless I am to stay on the bridge I must pass and be passed: it is easier to give a total refusal to love than to say in the same breath: "Come" and "Don't stay with me". Those who have been disillusioned with the love of creatures are those who wanted to make their dwelling on the bridge. They are wrong in thinking they have loved too much; what has happened is that their love has stood still.

*   *   *

The Channel and the Source.—If you seek *in* me you will find nothing. But everything—God included—can come *through* me. The mistake lies in seeing the creature as a source: the disillusionment that follows comes from not having perceived it is a channel.

*   *   *

Human love has its limits. Just as birth is the limit of the life of the embryo, so earthly life has eternity for its limit. A limit implies a transformation: every limit in love is an invitation to love *otherwise*. But man rejects these transformations; his love cleaves obstinately to its original form, refuses to die in order to live again—with the result that it dies altogether. The supreme achievement of that parasite in the human soul, whether we call it "sin" or "selfishness", is to make every moulting-season a death. The corpse of every dead affection is a metamorphosis miscarried.

* * *

Woe to him who has a longing and vocation for eternity and is yet unable to rise above time! According to the stamp of his character, or the object of his desire, he is either Prometheus or Alcestis, Tristan or Don Juan. He is for ever torn between the real and the impossible; he is for ever breaking bounds. Sometimes he thinks he is freeing himself; but there is no deliverance for him in this world; every craving to escape ends in a change of prison. There is one essential sin—perhaps it is the only one, for everything else we call sin is a mere breach of social rules, without transcendent importance. It is the attempt to slake an eternal thirst with draughts that are only temporal. This is the essence of tragedy, and of hell; to desire the infinite and remain captive to the finite, powerless to change anything in these conflicting appeals. Tragedy is not in time itself but in prostituting the eternal to time. There is nothing tragic about a worm crawling in the mud, because it was made for mud, and mud for it. But what is truly tragic is a wounded bird trailing its wings in the mud.

* * *

I see you as poor and frail, in peril, about to die. What makes my love for you so deep is the eternal destiny at the heart of it and the terrible certainty that you will die. It is only the knowledge that death is awaiting you that makes me love you with such infinite pity, with such an agony of hope. Yet what I love more than you is God, who is in peril of nothing. But God's dwelling is not only in heaven; he lives also in souls, and there is no life so fragile and perilous as that. Nothing in the world is so mortal as God in man, nothing so near to the point of death; the least shock of passion or self-interest, the least pressure of mean compliance, is enough to kill him. Here the supreme reality becomes as timorous and flimsy as a dream; and that is why the love of the saints is so tender, so shot with pity, for ever trembling between hope and fear. They have to defend their God every day against death.

*   *   *

DEATH AND LOVE.—If she were still alive our union would be perfect! But actually she is dead, she *cannot* live any more. It is this feeling of the irreparable that gives my idea of perfection the purity of despair, all its trenchant finality. My idea of perfection is suckled by the impossible. It was in losing you that I knew the uttermost depths of our love. It was your death that completely fitted me to possess you; by sweeping away the object it completed the *preparation* of the subject, it perfected my hunger as it robbed me of sustenance. The sight of this mortal

affinity that everywhere, in this world, weds fulfilment to the impossible raises a vital question, and
the answer to it decides the issue between living and
dead metaphysics: is death an obstacle that can be
overcome?

*   *   *

ABSENCE.—The day I failed to find you I did not
see the place where you were not: I did not see your
absence, I saw you absent. The object, even when
it is not there, comes first; the absence is something
secondary, a kind of flaw in the object itself. It is
not the absence of bread that is a torment to the
poor, but the bread that is missing, the desire that is
already the object itself—a restless, germinating,
imprisoned object, an object eager to be fulfilled and
to become incarnate. *Thirst is water disfigured.*
When I saw your face that was not present, that
means that what I saw before me was simply the
face of my desire—a face unhappy and imploring,
but still *your* face.

*   *   *

SUSPENSE.—Suspense is an unendurable tension
between the certainty of a love that is felt to be
eternal and the uncertainty of a physical presence
that is felt to be fleeting and imperilled. What
greater anguish than to feel substance at the mercy
of accident! Suspense is the feeling of necessity
enslaved to chance.

*   *   *

To the destroyer.—You who have created in me such discord, such frenzy and ruin, that I can never again find satisfaction in myself, or repose in any but an invulnerable peace—my blessings on you: you have saved me from happiness!

*　　*　　*

Autumn road.—Unloving, I made love, and vainly yearned for the springtime that was dead. Then I kissed her hand: it was cold as marble. And that was my very first kiss in eternity.